W9-DBK-497

**New Directions for
Institutional Research**

John F. Ryan
EDITOR-IN-CHIEF

Gloria Crisp
ASSOCIATE EDITOR

Emerging Research
and Practices on
First-Year Students

Ryan D. Padgett

EDITOR

Number 160
Jossey-Bass
San Francisco

882602331

EMERGING RESEARCH AND PRACTICES ON FIRST-YEAR STUDENTS
Ryan D. Padgett (ed.)
New Directions for Institutional Research, no. 160
John F. Ryan, Editor-in-Chief
Gloria Crisp, Associate Editor

NEW DIRECTIONS FOR INSTITUTIONAL RESEARCH (ISSN 0271-0579, electronic ISSN 1536-075X) is part of The Jossey-Bass Higher and Adult Education Series and is published quarterly by Wiley Subscription Services, Inc., A Wiley Company, at Jossey-Bass, One Montgomery Street, Suite 1200, San Francisco, California 94104-4594 (publication number USPS 098-830). POSTMASTER: Send address changes to New Directions for Institutional Research, Jossey-Bass, One Montgomery Street, Suite 1200, San Francisco, California 94104-4594.

INDIVIDUAL SUBSCRIPTION RATE (in USD): $89 per year US/Can/Mex, $113 rest of world; institutional subscription rate: $317 US, $357 Can/Mex, $391 rest of world. Single copy rate: $29. Electronic only–all regions: $89 individual, $317 institutional; Print & Electronic–US: $98 individual, $365 institutional; Print & Electronic–Canada/Mexico: $98 individual, $405 institutional; Print & Electronic–Rest of World: $122 individual, $439 institutional.

EDITORIAL CORRESPONDENCE should be sent to John F. Ryan at jfryan@uvm.edu.

New Directions for Institutional Research is indexed in _Academic Search_ (EBSCO), _Academic Search Elite_ (EBSCO), _Academic Search Premier_ (EBSCO), _CIJE: Current Index to Journals in Education_ (ERIC), _Contents Pages in Education_ (T&F), EBSCO Professional Development Collection (EBSCO), _Educational Research Abstracts Online_ (T&F), ERIC Database (Education Resources Information Center), _Higher Education Abstracts_ (Claremont Graduate University), _Multicultural Education Abstracts_ (T&F), _Sociology of Education Abstracts_ (T&F).

Microfilm copies of issues and chapters are available in 16mm and 35mm, as well as microfiche in 105mm, through University Microfilms, Inc., 300 North Zeeb Road, Ann Arbor, Michigan 48106-1346.

www.josseybass.com

THE ASSOCIATION FOR INSTITUTIONAL RESEARCH (AIR) is the world's largest professional association for institutional researchers. The organization provides educational resources, best practices, and professional development opportunities for more than 4,000 members. Its primary purpose is to support members in the process of collecting, analyzing, and converting data into information that supports decision making in higher education.

Contents

Editor's Notes   1
Ryan D. Padgett

1. Conceptual Considerations for First-Year Assessment   5
Jennifer R. Keup, Cindy A. Kilgo
This chapter provides a foundational understanding of first-year assessment as well as some considerations to help support key decisions in the assessment process of first-year experiences and programs.

2. High-Impact Practices and the First-Year Student   19
Malika Tukibayeva, Robert M. Gonyea
This chapter examines the relationships between empirically supported high-impact practices—service learning, learning communities, and research with faculty—and selected outcomes in the first year of college.

3. Good Practices for Whom? A Vital Question for   37
Understanding the First Year of College
Kathleen M. Goodman
Demonstrating the effects of good teaching and academic challenge on leadership and psychological well-being, this chapter reveals the importance of disaggregating data by race or other relevant characteristics when examining the impact of college on first-year students.

4. Programs and Practices That Retain Students From the First   53
to Second Year: Results From a National Study
Linda DeAngelo
Using data from a nationally representative longitudinal study, this chapter provides additional evidence into what types of first-year experiences affect persistence.

5. The First-Year Experience in Community Colleges   77
Trudy Bers, Donna Younger
This chapter provides a thorough examination of the characteristics of first-year experience programs in community colleges and the challenges in delivering these experiences in the two-year setting.

Index   95

EDITOR'S NOTES

Research on the first-year experience is as ubiquitous as the components of "the first-year experience." The myriad of research and assessment—both national and local—have produced a sort of internal debate within higher education as to the consistency of the findings and the success of their application to practice. Stated differently, initiatives that produce results on one campus may not on another. This inconsistency has ignited researchers to be more conscientious about assessing first-year experiences, as evident from the increase in quality data, applied complex statistical models, and assessment strategies within the literature.

Yet despite higher education's best efforts, pinpointing the exact means through which students succeed or persist on a four-year graduation track is as elusive as ever. With a greater diversity in the demographics of students, decreasing public appropriations, and calls for more stringent levels of accountability, research and assessment on the first year continues to be prevalent and relevant. In the face of these challenges, "institutions of higher education have increasingly embraced their obligation for assisting students with the transition to the college learning environment" (Swing, 2004, p. ix). To this end, this volume continues the examination of the first year and the factors that impact student success and persistence.

Together, the chapters within this volume provide a template for researchers on the statistical methods that need to be considered when conducting assessment on first-year experiences. Chapter 1 provides a comprehensive blueprint outlining the foundational understandings of first-year assessment. Grounded in the conceptual framework of sound assessment, Chapter 1 provides novice and intermediate researchers with a firm understanding of the decisions to consider prior to assessment. Chapters 2–4 utilize large, national surveys to examine the impact of the first year on a variety of learning and retention outcomes. Chapter 2 highlights three first-year programs (e.g., high-impact practices) that statistically increase student learning. Chapter 3 expands upon the programs of the first year by estimating the effects of vetted good practices across two psychosocial measures. In addition, Chapter 3 provides a sound argument for the need to disaggregate data across student characteristics to more accurately assess the impact of these practices across groups. Chapter 4 provides a comprehensive predictive model, illustrating the importance of the use of control and covariate measures to estimate student persistence. Finally, Chapter 5 expands our understanding of the first-year experience by documenting the challenges of applying these experiences within two-year institutions.

Before practitioners can utilize data-driven processes, sound empirical evidence must be collected. The question as to "where to begin?" is

NEW DIRECTIONS FOR INSTITUTIONAL RESEARCH, no. 160 © 2014 Wiley Periodicals, Inc.
Published online in Wiley Online Library (wileyonlinelibrary.com) • DOI: 10.1002/ir.20057

thoroughly discussed in Chapter 1. Jennifer R. Keup and Cindy A. Kilgo provide one of the more compelling and comprehensive examinations of assessment techniques. Supported by recent research, Keup and Kilgo provide a road map for emerging researchers on first-year assessment as well as considerations to help support these decisions.

Over the last decade, research on high-impact practices has become as prevalent as research on first-year experiences. Yet despite the overwhelmingly positive evidence, few have isolated the effects of high-impact practices within the first year. Using data from the National Survey of Student Engagement, Malika Tukibayeva and Robert M. Gonyea estimate the impact of first-year participation in service learning, learning communities, and research with faculty on student learning. Critical to this evaluation is the snapshot of participation broken down by student and institutional characteristics.

The assessment movement within higher education has relied heavily on longitudinal studies to accurately estimate student learning and development. Using data from the Wabash National Study of Liberal Arts Education, Kathleen M. Goodman presents a strong argument for the necessity to disaggregate data by student characteristics when measuring the effects of a program/practice on any outcome. If the ultimate goal for a researcher is to accurately measure the impact of participation and engagement, Goodman suggests that disaggregating data or accounting for conditional effects must become routine.

There is no magic potion with regard to fully understanding student persistence. However, the soundness of the analyses and statistical model are vital to the success of accurate estimates of college impact. Linda DeAngelo illustrates how to construct a strong and accurate model for prediction by accounting for prior research and utilizing valid controls and covariates. Using data from the Cooperative Institutional Research Program's 2007 Freshman Survey and 2008 Your First College Year survey, DeAngelo walks through the creation of a prediction model and how the findings can influence future models and practice.

The overwhelming majority of research on first-year experiences has been limited to four-year institutions. Trudy Bers and Donna Younger examine the first-year experience but apply the experiences within the two-year setting. In addition to providing an overview of the literature, Bers and Younger discuss how the research can be integrated within community colleges and the challenges of delivering these programs and assessing them. The incorporation of this chapter within this volume advances the argument that first-year experiences are just as important and influential on two-year campuses as they are on four-year campuses.

By no means does the concentration of these chapters dedicated to first-year experiences indicate the end of such research. Arguably, the culmination of this research has generated practical debate on how to best serve and support student learning, development, and success. Together, these chapters serve to enlighten the discussion and highlight new directions for assessment and research practices within the scope of the first-year experience.

Ryan D. Padgett
Editor

Reference

Swing, R. L. (2004). *Proving and improving, Volume II: Tools and techniques for assessing the first college year* (Monograph No. 37). Columbia: University of South Carolina, National Resource Center for The First-Year Experience and Students in Transition.

RYAN D. PADGETT, PhD, *is the assistant vice president for student success and assessment in the Division of Student Affairs at Northern Kentucky University.*

NEW DIRECTIONS FOR INSTITUTIONAL RESEARCH • DOI: 10.1002/ir

1

Supported by emerging research and practice, this chapter provides a comprehensive conceptual framework for first-year assessment.

Conceptual Considerations for First-Year Assessment

Jennifer R. Keup, Cindy A. Kilgo

For decades, issues surrounding student access and success have been of perennial interest to college educators and researchers, and the first year of college has been recognized as both the springboard for student achievement and success and a significant leakage point in the educational pipeline. Recently, the early success of first-year students has taken on even greater importance due to changes in the higher education landscape, including demands from regional accrediting agencies for more accountability, shifting demographics, differential success rates among new student populations, and a realization on the part of institutions about the importance—both financially and in meeting their commitment to students—of retaining their currently enrolled undergraduates. As such, institutional budget officers, policy makers, and others who invest in first-year student success are searching for research and resources to help inform data-driven decision making about promising practices to support the adjustment and success of first-year students and the effective use of high-impact educational experiences and practices in first-year experience programs.

Institutional assessment activities focused on first-year students have been both the impetus and response to this emphasis on first-year student success and first-year experience programs. Assessment data collected from first-year students are able to serve a wide range of purposes. They can provide an understanding of the background, characteristics, and needs of the student cohort; gauge satisfaction with their college choice and experiences; provide perceptions of campus climate from the newest members of the campus community; evaluate the impact and cost-effectiveness of first-year programs and initiatives; measure student learning outcomes and program outcomes; and create benchmarks against comparable institutions, an aspirant group, or nationally accepted standards (Schuh, 2005; Siegel, 2003; Swing, 2004; Upcraft, 2004). Further, empirical data collected from students throughout their first year in college have great utility with respect

New Directions for Institutional Research, no. 160 © 2014 Wiley Periodicals, Inc.
Published online in Wiley Online Library (wileyonlinelibrary.com) • DOI: 10.1002/ir.20058

to their timing in the trajectory of student performance and success. For example, first-year assessment activity can generate follow-up data to outreach and admissions efforts as a posttest. However, they also provide baseline data, or a pretest, for the curricular and cocurricular experiences in students' first year and beyond that are intended to enhance the cognitive, affective, and interpersonal development of college undergraduates.

And yet, the power of first-year assessment data to enhance programs, pedagogies, and policies for first-year students is dependent upon effective strategies and decisions within the data collection, analysis, and dissemination process. While in certain instances there are clear "right" and "wrong" choices, more often, higher education assessment activity is comprised of subtle, nuanced judgments that are dependent upon a number of other factors. In sum, assessment of students, programs, and outcomes represents a web of decisions. This chapter attempts to address a few of the more common "forks in the assessment pathway" in an effort to provide a foundational understanding of first-year assessment activities as well as some considerations to help support key decisions within that process. National data on institutional assessment practices for first-year initiatives punctuate the discussion, illustrate the national trends and issues with respect to first-year assessment, and provide a broader context for institutional assessment decisions. However, the overall goal of this chapter is to provide a conceptual framework for first-year assessment as a scaffold for more sophisticated statistical and methodological aspects of assessment practice. In particular, this chapter addresses (a) the match between objectives and outcomes, (b) quantitative, qualitative, and mixed methodologies, (c) national surveys and locally developed assessment instruments, and (d) direct and indirect measures.

Objectives and Outcomes

First-year assessment activities can take a number of forms and pursue a range of purposes. However, the rise in national attention to accountability in higher education, institutional efforts for data-driven decision making, and return on resource investment have brought greater attention to outcome assessment. As such, the evaluation of impact on outcomes is often the primary focus of assessment strategies in undergraduate education overall and the first-year experience in particular. Such endeavors attempt to address "What happened?" and "What mattered?" (Ewell, 2001, p. 3) leading ultimately to "the most fundamental question of all: Is what we are doing [for first-year students] having any effect, and is that effect the intended one?" (Upcraft, 2004, p. 478).

For most outcome assessment processes to be effective, they must draw from clearly defined purposes and goals of the initiative under evaluation (Huba & Freed, 2000; Maki, 2002; Upcraft, Crissman Ishler, & Swing, 2004). Much like a journey without a destination is likely to be inefficient and ineffective, without identifying the desired outcomes of a student success effort, assessment results are likely to reveal a lack of cohesiveness and impact. Common objectives for first-year student initiatives represent long-standing and perennial outcomes of interest to higher education such as retention, satisfaction, and grade point average. However, these measures are more frequently complemented by broader learning objectives that are "developmental or emergent over time," "more complex and sophisticated," and focused on fostering "robust learning" skills rather than sole reliance upon specific subject-knowledge acquisition, personal satisfaction, or persistence (Rhodes, 2010, p. 1). These "21st century learning outcomes" represent "a powerful core of knowledge and capacities that all student should acquire" to become "intentional learners, self-aware about the reasons for their studies, adaptable in using knowledge, and able to connect seemingly disparate experiences" (Leskes & Miller, 2006, p. 2). For example, national data on first-year program and assessment outcomes include academic, personal, civic, and interpersonal engagement and skill development; clearer understanding of the purposes of higher education, general education, and liberal arts; intercultural competence and global citizenship; and appreciation of interdisciplinary perspectives, in addition to more traditional measures such as persistence to the second year; improved academic performance and achievement; sense of belonging; satisfaction with the institution, classes, faculty, and peer connections; and knowledge and use of campus resources (Barefoot & Koch, 2011; Padgett & Keup, 2011).

The identification and expansion of first-year outcomes to more current definitions of learning and development represent a promising practice in first-year experience programming and assessment. However, progress is hampered by a disconnect between these inclusive outcomes and the measures employed in assessment strategies. Multifarious measures that directly gauge knowledge and skills—such as rubrics, portfolios, and capstone projects—are influential in effectively assessing learning objectives. Too often, program objectives represent articulation of broad learning objectives but the assessment strategy relies upon transactional measures that do not adequately capture progress and achievement of student learning and program goals.

Data from the 2009 National Survey of First-Year Seminars, administered by the National Resource Center for The First-Year Experience and Students in Transition, provide an example of this disconnect between learning/program objectives and assessment outcomes (Padgett & Keup, 2011). Eight hundred and fifty-seven institutions provided information about their first-year seminars, which included their most important course objectives. The top objectives were:

- Develop academic skills
- Develop a connection with the institution
- Provide orientation to campus resources and services

- Self-exploration/personal development
- Create common first-year experience
- Develop support network/friendships

However, information collected about the measures and outcomes of assessment activities revealed a very different picture of priorities. Almost three quarters of these survey respondents reported that they measured first-to-second year persistence as an outcome of first-year seminars, but only 15.5% of respondents identified this measure as one of their three most important course objectives. It is also interesting to note that more than 70% of institutions participating in the national survey measured satisfaction with faculty as a seminar outcome, but fewer than 20% prioritized increased student/faculty interaction among their top course objectives. Similarly, there was a 15.1 percentage-point gap between the proportion of survey respondents that measured satisfaction with the institution as a first-year seminar outcome (65.3%) and the percent that reported that developing a connection with the institution was an important course objective (50.2%).

In order to truly inform the relevance and excellence of the first-year student success initiatives such as first-year seminars, it is critical that assessment strategies measure the stated objectives of the program. While not conclusive evidence, the statistics generated by the 2009 National Survey of First-Year Seminars suggest institutional overreliance upon easily acquired assessment outcomes, such as retention rates and satisfaction measures, regardless of their alignment with the stated objectives for the seminar and true measurement of student development and learning.

Quantitative, Qualitative, and Mixed Methodologies

Another key decision in a first-year assessment pertains to the selection of methodology and the resultant type of data. All inquiry, including assessment and research, draws from two methodological approaches: qualitative and quantitative. These assessment perspectives are often discussed as if they represent an "either/or" scenario. However, each approach has its own strengths, is appropriate to the study of first-year students, and can be used in combination as a part of mixed-methodology studies.

As a review of its most basic tenets, qualitative methodology collects data about the meaning of events and activities to the people involved. This assessment approach is concerned with understanding the individual within a particular context, and thus the findings generated from these data are not intended to be generalizable. Instead, qualitative inquiry seeks to "achieve an understanding of how people make sense out of their lives, to delineate the process (rather than the outcome or product) of meaning making, and to describe how people interpret what they experience" (Merriam & Simpson, 2000, p. 97). Most often, the data collected by these means are narrative and commonly gathered via individual interviews, focus groups (i.e., group interviews), written responses to open-ended survey items, document analyses, and journals. However, qualitative data can also be gathered visually via observation of student behavior in classrooms, student life, and performances or captured in portfolios, reflective photography, or other forms of artistic expression. These data are then analyzed to find themes and nonstatistical relationships and patterns. While certainly informed by the assessment outcomes, the process of analysis and data distillation in qualitative assessment is typically inductive in nature and builds meaning and theory from the research procedure itself.

The purpose of quantitative methodology is to describe what is occurring; test relationships between individuals, programs, environments, and outcomes; and determine causality of events and effects upon the outcome of interest. In short, it seeks to answer the questions: (a) what is happening? and (b) what caused it? Quantitative data are numerical and most frequently drawn from surveys and analyses of existing data such as those drawn from the admissions office, campus registrar, utilization statistics, placement testing, advising and counseling offices, and course/program evaluation processes. Because quantitative methodology seeks to identify potentially causal relationships between variables and to test certain conditions and outcomes, these assessment procedures are typically deductive and product-oriented, rather than process-oriented. Quantitative analysis uses statistics to test assumptions, to predict behavior and outcomes, and to determine the impact of programs, experiences, and intentional interventions.

Historically, quantitative data have been used far more frequently in higher education institutional research and assessment than qualitative data. The vast stores of quantitative data already in our assessment coffers from typical institutional transactions, coupled with availability of national survey assessment tools and the ease of collecting data via institutional questionnaires, have caused quantitative data to dominate the first-year assessment scene. However, over the past 10 years, qualitative methodology has gained a strong foothold in higher education assessment in general and the first-year experience in particular. Several national qualitative studies and resources related to first-year initiatives and outcomes helped bring greater emphasis to this methodology. These include the case study approach of the Documenting Effective Educational Practice (DEEP) project conducted by the Center for Postsecondary Research at Indiana University (Kuh, Kinzie, Schuh, Whitt, & Associates, 2005), aspects of the self-study component of the Foundations of Excellence process sponsored by the John N. Gardner Institute for Excellence in Undergraduate Education (Alexander & Gardner, 2009), Valid Assessment of Learning in Undergraduate Education (VALUE) rubrics created by the Association of American Colleges and Universities (AAC&U) to assess learning across a spectrum of "21st century learning outcomes" (Rhodes, 2010), and the qualitative component of the Wabash National Study of Liberal Arts Education conducted by researchers at the University of Michigan and Miami University in collaboration with colleagues at the Center of Inquiry in the Liberal Arts at Wabash College and the University of Iowa (Goodman, Baxter Magolda, Seifert, & King, 2011). The examples provided by the qualitative or mixed-methodology approach in these studies coupled with advancements in the variety of qualitative methods and analytical tools have helped expand this approach in first-year assessment practices.

Data drawn from the 2009 National Survey of First-Year Seminars provide important information about the use of both qualitative and quantitative data in the assessment activities of the most commonly used first-year initiative (Padgett & Keup, 2011). The 475 survey responses from institutional representatives about first-year seminar assessment methods indicated that quantitative assessment strategies were used more frequently than qualitative methods. More specifically, the overwhelming majority of respondents from this sample (95%) reported that they used the quantitative data drawn from student course evaluations in their assessment plan. Further, three quarters of respondents indicated that they used a survey instrument in their assessment of the course, and a nearly identical proportion reported that they conducted secondary analyses of institutional data to evaluate first-year seminar outcomes. These statistics remained consistent when the data were disaggregated by institutional type (i.e., two-year or four-year campus), institutional control (public vs. private), and size of first-year cohort, thereby suggesting that these three examples of quantitative data—course evaluations, survey instruments, and analyses of institutional data—are becoming fixtures in the assessment practices for first-year seminars. Further, these assessment practices are likely to serve as a model for assessment activities in other curricular and cocurricular first-year student support initiatives across all types of colleges and universities.

Although not as widespread as quantitative methodologies, the use of qualitative data to assess first-year seminars was also reported among many respondents to the 2009 national survey (Padgett & Keup, 2011). Forty-three percent of the sample indicated that they conducted focus groups with students in the seminars and 30% hosted individual interviews to collect qualitative feedback from the students in these courses. Further, qualitative methodologies were the primary means by which instructor feedback was included in the assessment activities for first-year seminars. A greater proportion of survey respondents indicated that they used individual or group interviews for first-year seminar faculty than they did for the students: 51% of the sample reported conducting focus groups with instructors and 46% stated that they employed interviews with instructors as an assessment strategy. Given that faculty, staff, and administrators are not often represented in quantitative first-year assessment plans and only occasionally included in quantitative tools, qualitative data may represent an important means of including the evaluative feedback of other campus constituencies that are intimately connected to the success of first-year students.

NEW DIRECTIONS FOR INSTITUTIONAL RESEARCH • DOI: 10.1002/ir

These data indicate that the evolution of qualitative methodologies in first-year assessment has done more than just highlight such inquiry as a stand-alone assessment practice for the first-year experience. Qualitative methodology is regularly used to complement quantitative assessment strategies to triangulate findings, include voices not represented in the quantitative approaches, and provide depth of understanding to survey results on first-year experiences and outcomes. As such, the combination of quantitative and qualitative approaches in mixed-methodology studies incorporates multiple views and multiple sources to help document, explain, and enhance the first-year experience and, thus, has become one of the hallmarks of high-quality first-year assessment (see Barefoot et al., 2005; Swing, 2004; Upcraft, 2004).

National Surveys and Locally Developed Assessment Instruments

While qualitative methodology has gained a strong foothold in first-year assessment and institutional research practices, quantitative methods, most notably surveys, are still the primary means of collecting large amounts of student data in an efficient and resource-effective manner. Over the past few decades, the increased demand for accountability in higher education has led to the proliferation of national survey instruments as well as enhanced tools for the development and analysis of institutional assessment efforts. While the large number of surveys and services can be beneficial to institutional assessment efforts during the first year, it also can be overwhelming and complicate the decision about whether to participate in national survey efforts or to develop an institutional, or "local," assessment tool.

The acronyms of national surveys such as CIRP, NSSE, CCSSE, LASSI, CSEQ, CSI, and PEEK relevant to the first-year experience create a virtual alphabet soup of options, which can be used in a number of ways to assess the first-year experience. The breadth of options of national survey tools is such that there is likely a survey already in existence for nearly every first-year assessment need. Swing (2004) proposed a typology of such first-year survey instruments to help organize the multitude of options, which includes surveys that collect preenrollment or baseline data; experiences and outcomes of the first college year; general student experience surveys; information on specific first-year services, units, and programs; data on specific first-year student populations; and information on academic knowledge for the purposes of placement.

National survey instruments also offer benefits beyond merely providing options for a range of first-year assessment needs. Use of an existing national instrument saves valuable time and resources in the survey development phase of the assessment process (Schuh, Upcraft, & Associates, 2001). Further, most national instruments have been fully vetted and are psychometrically sound, thereby maximizing the validity and reliability of the assessment data that they generate (Swing, 2004; Swing & Upcraft, 2004). National survey tools often include detailed guidelines for administration and automated means for harvesting, cleaning, and scoring the data that they collect, which address two of the most common barriers to assessment: lack of assessment expertise and lack of professional staff support (Upcraft, 2004). Finally, national assessment tools allow for the comparison of an institution's data to a set of peers, aspirant group, or national results to help interpret campus findings within the larger landscape of higher education. This tendency to examine first-year students, their experiences, and the effectiveness of institutional interventions through benchmarking against the performance of other institutions in these domains is identified as a standard of excellence in first-year practices. More specifically, Barefoot et al. (2005) concluded from their in-depth study of 13 institutions with highly effective first-year programs that "a central component of excellence is a steady outward gaze—the willingness to learn from and share with others" (p. 390) of which assessment data generated via national surveys are critically important.

The incredible array of commercially developed assessment tools and the host of benefits that they offer provide a compelling argument for a first-year assessment plan comprised entirely of such national assessment tools. Yet, eschewing locally developed assessment tools is not always the firm rule of first-year assessment. The purpose of the assessment study and the outcomes of interest are paramount to the selection of the data collection method and tool and should not be subverted in order to participate in a national survey. Despite the broad selection base of first-year assessment tools, if there is no commercially developed survey available that fits the intention of the study, a well-developed, psychometrically sound, locally developed instrument is the only viable option (Swing & Upcraft, 2004). In addition, assessment is fundamentally a political activity that is firmly rooted in the history, culture, and leadership of an institution and driven by the interests of internal constituencies as much as, or even more than, audiences external to the college or university (El-Khawas, 1991; Schuh & Upcraft, 2000; Upcraft, 2004). These realities may require a data collection instrument more attuned to the elements of organizational climate and campus constituencies than national surveys are able to achieve. This is especially true when the higher education institution, new student cohort, strategic planning activities, and/or first-year programs are more specialized or innovative. These conditions often require that campus leaders and assessment professionals establish their own internal benchmarks for achievement as well as develop corresponding surveys to appropriately measure progress and success. It is important to note, however, that institution-specific assessment activities do not have to be conducted from scratch. Much like the marketplace for national survey tools, there are a number of commercially developed services and resources to assist in the development of institution-specific surveys that range from published guidelines for the consideration and creation of survey items to platforms for online survey development and administration to various consultation options for campus-specific first-year assessment plans.

Again, recent data collected by the National Resource Center for The First-Year Experience and Students in Transition on the assessment activities for first-year seminars provide a prime example of how institutions across the country are making decisions about the use of national assessment instruments and/or locally developed surveys (Padgett & Keup, 2011). Of the 475 institutions reporting that they engaged in assessment activities for their first-year seminars, respondents from 357 campuses reported that they used survey instruments in their assessment plan, which was second only to course evaluations as the most common method of assessing these seminars. Interestingly, despite the burgeoning number of national assessment tools on the first-year experience and first-year seminars, the most popular type of survey for first-year seminar assessment was one that was developed locally; 84% of the respondents that administered a survey stated that they used such a "homegrown" survey. Just over half of the same group of respondents indicated that they used a national survey to assess the seminar and students' experiences in the course, thereby revealing a significant number of institutions that utilized both national and locally developed instruments. Additional survey data showed that common national surveys used to assess first-year seminars included the National Survey of Student Engagement (NSSE) sponsored by the Center for Postsecondary Research at Indiana University, the Community College Survey of Student Engagement (CCSSE) housed in the Community College Leadership Program at the University of Texas at Austin, the Freshman Survey and Your First College Year (YFCY) survey offered by the Cooperative Institutional Research Program (CIRP) at UCLA, and the First-Year Initiative (FYI) survey sponsored by Educational Benchmarking Inc. (EBI), although these were far from the only surveys identified as national measurement tools used for first-year seminar assessment (Padgett & Keup, 2011).

Therefore, while institutional research and assessment scholars tout the strengths of using national tools in good practices for assessment of the first-year experience, national data indicate that locally developed institution-specific surveys are still widely used. Perhaps even more telling is the fact that campuses appear to be using both types of surveys to strengthen their assessment findings for first-year seminars and, very likely, other first-year and student success programs. It is likely that the political nature of assessment, the continued presence of national assessment tools in the academic marketplace, and the demand for multiple measures of accountability will combine as forces to encourage campuses to use both national and locally developed assessment tools in their first-year assessment activities.

Direct and Indirect Measures

Two primary types of measures—direct and indirect—can be utilized within both quantitative and qualitative student success assessment efforts. While moderate debate has transpired regarding whether direct and indirect measures share equal validity from a statistical perspective (Gonyea, 2005), both direct and indirect measures serve respective roles within the evaluation of student learning outcomes. Exploring the characteristics of direct and indirect measures, as well as the possible uses for each, can assist in the decision to employ either or both within first-year assessment endeavors.

Direct measures seek to attain data in an objective manner. They do not rely upon self-reported or perceived changes for various outcomes; instead, they require demonstration of the skills, abilities, knowledge, or development as a result of students' participation in specific programs, use of a service or resource, or involvement within the first-year experience. Some examples of methods for directly measuring learning outcomes include exams, portfolios, projects, standardized tests, common assignments, examinations of written work, and performances (see Banta, Jones, & Black, 2009; Maki, 2002; Palomba, 2001). The primary benefit of direct measures is that they gather data with high impartiality, thereby lessening the amount of variance and increasing the validity of the data that they collect. While the value of direct measures is apparent, they are not without limitations, including their difficulty to capture data, the introduction of bias, and their labor and cost intensity. For example, standardized testing is a direct measure that receives ongoing scrutiny for its inability to accurately and efficiently measure learning across a diversity of students on a standardized scale (see Fleming & Garcia, 1998; Gonyea, 2005; Haladyna, 2006). Other types of direct measures, such as portfolios, presentations, and performances, can provide information that can easily estimate achievement toward learning outcomes (Palomba, 2001), but are often time and resource intensive.

Indirect measures, commonly referred to as self-reported measures, attain data in a subjective manner, in which students self-report information or perceived changes in outcomes. A few examples of methods for indirectly measuring learning outcomes include satisfaction measures, self-rating of skills, self-assessment of change, level of agreement with value statements, and program or course evaluations (Maki, 2002; Palomba, 2001). Indirect measures are typically easier and more cost efficient to employ than direct measures (Gonyea, 2005) and are often correlated to varying degrees with direct measures. Thus, they compose a large proportion of measures implemented within college research and assessment, including the first year (Pascarella, 2001b). Further, indirect measures also allow for the assessment of outcomes that cannot be addressed directly (Gonyea, 2005), most notably those that are affective and psychological in nature (Astin, 1991). Some examples of such outcomes that are often a component of first-year programming include clarity of values, motivation, self-understanding, identity development, multicultural competence, academic and career interests, and sense of belonging.

Despite these benefits, the greatest limitation to indirect measures is their validity and reliability. Indirect measures do not, in fact, provide evidence of knowledge acquisition or skill development. Instead, data generated via indirect measures only confirm that the subject *perceives* that such gains took place. Wording of survey questions and statements can vary in the level of factual response requested, which has the potential to positively impact the psychometric soundness of data collected via indirect measures (Gonyea, 2005; Pascarella, 2001a). For example, significant variation in responses can exist when surveys include questions or statements asking respondents to report their perceived change due to an experience or variable. Further, other assessment strategies can be used to add validity to studies using indirect measures, such as pretest/posttest design or control variables (see Pascarella, 2001a, 2001b). If implemented efficiently, indirect measures are able to produce data that can serve as a useful, efficient, and cost-effective resource within the assessment plan for student success and learning in the first year.

Data from the National Survey of First-Year Seminars (Padgett & Keup, 2011) and the National Survey of Efforts to Improve Undergraduate Student Success and Retention conducted by the John N. Gardner Institute for Excellence in Undergraduate Education (Barefoot & Koch, 2011) provide illustrations of how direct and indirect measures are incorporated into first-year assessment plans. Perhaps not surprisingly, the most consistently employed assessment measures were direct measures of retention (to the sophomore year and to graduation) and grade point average. Other common direct measures included utilization statistics for campus services, participation in campus activities and events, and other measures of academic achievement such as conferment of honors and development of major-related competencies. Direct measures of student learning or skill development were mentioned far less frequently, although items on both surveys drew some mention of achievement of learning or course outcomes, enhancement of writing ability, development of critical thinking, career readiness, greater understanding of linkages between disciplines, and civic engagement. Conversely, satisfaction measures dominated the list of indirect measures used among respondents to the 2009 administration of the National Survey of First-Year Seminars, including satisfaction with faculty, the institution, advising, campus services, or courses. Other examples of indirect measures used to assess first-year seminars and other undergraduate student success initiatives from both national surveys include students' perceptions of course impact; self-reports of skill development; self-ratings of students' understanding of institutional identity and culture; and feelings of connection with peers, staff, and faculty.

Much like mixed-methodology assessment strategies, endeavors encompassing both direct measures and indirect measures are common (Banta et al., 2009). In fact, assessment initiatives that combine direct and indirect measures can provide a more holistic view of achievement toward learning outcomes. While both direct measures and indirect measures each have potential downfalls, they also can be implemented in a method that allows for valid and attainable results tailored for specific institution- or department-level needs. Direct measures generally provide an objective portrayal of learning, while indirect measures typically are less time consuming to administer. However, both direct and indirect measures are feasible and valuable tools within assessment. Creating and facilitating efficient instruments or techniques to measure learning outcomes requires a thorough examination of resources available (including time and finances), the environment in which the assessment measure can be used (e.g., online/web-based, in-person, within a classroom setting), the possibility of a pretest/posttest design being implemented, and the particular learning outcomes being assessed. Remembering not to confine indirect measures and direct measures as only employable under certain conditions is also important to consider when deciding which measure to use (see Palomba, 2001). Careful thinking regarding the best method of assessing student learning can assist in the decision of whether a direct measure, an indirect measure, or a combination of the two will best gauge student progress toward the stated outcomes.

Conclusion

This chapter highlights a number of key decision points in the process of first-year assessment that provide the foundation for a well-conceptualized and efficiently executed plan for institutional research in the first college year. For instance, careful consideration of the alignment between program/student learning objectives and assessment outcomes allows campus professionals to structure assessment activities that collect appropriate data and generate meaningful findings. Further, successful first-year assessment activity is contingent upon thoughtful reflection, selection, and combination of methodology, instruments, and measures within the framework of those objectives and outcomes.

First-year assessment activity, particularly program and learning outcome assessment, is critical to documenting student learning and development; program development, administration, and improvement; and showing evidence of institutional effectiveness and accountability. As the number of assessment resources, methodologies, measures, and outcomes evolve, we are witnessing more blended approaches to assessment strategies. Whatever the outcome of the various decisions inherent in any first-year assessment plan, it is most critical that assessment continues to take place. National data reveal that between 30% and 40% of institutions do not regularly assess their student success initiatives and, thus, cannot reliably comment upon their impact or outcome achievement (see Barefoot & Koch, 2011;

Padgett & Keup, 2011). Too often, institutions cut assessment activities and rely upon anecdotal data in the interest of saving resources. In truth, sound investment and stewardship of resources is dependent upon data-informed decision making.

References

Alexander, J. S., & Gardner, J. N. (2009). Beyond retention: A comprehensive approach to the first college year. *About Campus, 14*(2), 18–26.

Astin, A. W. (1991). *Assessment for excellence*. Phoenix, AZ: The Oryx Press.

Banta, T. W., Jones, E. A., & Black, K. E. (2009). *Designing effective assessment: Principles and profiles of good practice*. San Francisco, CA: Jossey-Bass.

Barefoot, B. O., Gardner, J. N., Cutright, M., Morris, L. V., Schroeder, C. C., Schwarts, S. W., . . . Swing, R. L. (2005). *Achieving and sustaining institutional excellence for the first year of college*. San Francisco, CA: Jossey-Bass.

Barefoot, B. O., & Koch, A. K. (2011, June). *Preliminary findings from a national survey of efforts to improve undergraduate student success and retention*. Presentation at the 24th International Conference on The First-Year Experience, Manchester, UK.

El-Khawas, E. (1991). Assessment on campus: Local instruments are strongly preferred. *Assessment Update, 3*(1), 4–5.

Ewell, P. T. (2001). Observations on assessing the first-year experience. In R. L. Swing (Ed.), *Proving and improving strategies for assessing the first college year* (pp. 3–5). Columbia, SC: National Resource Center for The First-Year Experience and Students in Transition.

Fleming, J., & Garcia, N. (1998). Are standardized tests fair to African Americans? Predictive validity of the SAT in black and white institutions. *The Journal of Higher Education, 69*(5), 471–495.

Gonyea, R. M. (2005). Self-reported data in institutional research: Review and recommendations. In P. D. Umbach (Ed.), *New Directions for Institutional Research: No. 127. Survey research: Emerging issues* (pp. 73–89). San Francisco, CA: Jossey-Bass.

Goodman, K. M., Baxter Magolda, M., Seifert, T. A., & King, P. M. (2011). Good practices for student learning: Mixed-method evidence from the Wabash National Study. *About Campus, 16*(1), 2–9.

Haladyna, T. M. (2006). Perils of standardized achievement testing. *Educational Horizons, 85*(1), 30–43.

Huba, M. E., & Freed, J. E. (2000). Learner centered assessment on college campuses: Shifting the focus from teaching to learning. *Community College Journal of Research and Practice, 24*(9), 759–766.

Kuh, G. D., Kinzie, J., Schuh, J. H., Whitt, E. J., & Associates. (2005). *Student success in college: Creating conditions that matter*. San Francisco, CA: Jossey-Bass.

Leskes, A., & Miller, R. (2006). *Purposeful pathways: Helping students achieve key learning outcomes*. Washington, DC: Association of American Colleges and Universities.

Maki, P. (2002, January). Using multiple assessment methods to explore student learning and development inside and outcome of the classroom. *NetResults*. Retrieved from http://www.apu.edu/live_data/files/333/multiple_assessment_methods_to_explore _student_learning_and_deve.pdf

Merriam, S. B., & Simpson, E. L. (2000). *A guide to research for educators and trainers of adults* (2nd ed. with updated material). Malabar, FL: Krieger Publishing Company.

Padgett, R. D., & Keup, J. R. (2011). *2009 National Survey of First-Year Seminars: Ongoing efforts to support students in transition*. Columbia, SC: University of South Carolina, National Resource Center for The First-Year Experience and Students in Transition.

Palomba, C. A. (2001). Implementing effective assessment. In C. A. Palomba & T. W. Banta (Eds.), *Assessing student competence in accredited disciplines: Pioneering approaches to assessment in higher education* (pp. 13–28). Sterling, VA: Stylus.

Pascarella, E. T. (2001a). Identifying excellence in undergraduate education: Are we even close? *Change, 33*(3), 19–23.

Pascarella, E. T. (2001b). Using student self-reported gains to estimate college impact: A cautionary tale. *Journal of College Student Development, 42*(5), 488–492.

Rhodes, T. L. (2010). *Assessing outcomes and improving achievement: Tips and tools for using rubrics.* Washington, DC: Association of American Colleges and Universities.

Schuh, J. H. (2005). Assessing programs and other student experiences designed to enrich the first-year experience. In R. S. Feldman (Ed.), *Improving the first year of college: Research and practice* (pp. 135–150). Mahwah, NJ: Lawrence Erlbaum Associates.

Schuh, J. H., & Upcraft, M. L. (2000). Assessment politics. *About Campus, 5*(4), 14–21.

Schuh, J. H., Upcraft, M. L., & Associates. (2001). *Assessment practice in student affairs: An applications manual.* San Francisco, CA: Jossey-Bass.

Siegel, M. J. (2003). *Primer on assessment of the first college year.* Brevard, NC: Policy Center on the First Year of College.

Swing, R. L. (2004). *Proving and improving, Volume II: Tools and techniques for assessing the first college year* (Monograph No. 37). Columbia, SC: University of South Carolina, National Resource Center for The First-Year Experience and Students in Transition.

Swing, R. L., & Upcraft, M. L. (2004). Choosing and using assessment instruments. In M. L. Upcraft, J. N. Gardner, B. O. Barefoot, & Associates (Eds.), *Challenging and supporting the first-year student: A handbook for improving the first year of college* (pp. 501–514). San Francisco, CA: Jossey-Bass.

Upcraft, M. L. (2004). Assessing the first year of college. In M. L. Upcraft, J. N. Gardner, B. O. Barefoot, & Associates (Eds.), *Challenging and supporting the first-year student: A handbook for improving the first year of college* (pp. 469–485). San Francisco, CA: Jossey-Bass.

Upcraft, M. L., Crissman Ishler, J. L., & Swing, R. L. (2004). A beginner's guide for assessing the first college year. In M. L. Upcraft, J. N. Gardner, B. O. Barefoot, & Associates (Eds.), *Challenging and supporting the first-year student: A handbook for improving the first year of college* (pp. 486–500). San Francisco, CA: Jossey-Bass.

JENNIFER R. KEUP *is the director of the National Resource Center for The First-Year Experience and Students in Transition and an affiliated faculty member in the Department of Educational Leadership and Policies in the College of Education at the University of South Carolina.*

CINDY A. KILGO *is a higher education and student affairs doctoral student and serves as a research assistant for the Center for Research on Undergraduate Education at The University of Iowa.*

2

High-impact practices, programs, and activities where students commit considerable time and effort in different settings can help to define the first-year college experience and are likely to increase success in areas like persistence, deep learning, and self-reported gains.

High-Impact Practices and the First-Year Student

Malika Tukibayeva, Robert M. Gonyea

The term *high-impact practices* is relatively new in the ongoing conversation about what matters in undergraduate learning, but the activities themselves have been promoted for decades. They include learning community programs which foster a sense of belongingness for students who are new to college and service-learning programs where students are challenged to test ideas from their coursework in real, unscripted community settings. High-impact practices also include experiences like conducting independent research with a supervising faculty member, first-year seminars, studying abroad, working on a career-enhancing internship, and completing a capstone or other type of culminating senior experience (Kuh, 2008).

First used by George Kuh in 2007 (National Survey of Student Engagement [NSSE], 2007), the term *high-impact practices* encompasses a variety of educational programs that make a difference in students' lives, bring substantial educational benefits, and correlate with better retention and engagement (Kuh, 2008). For example, learning communities, research with faculty, study abroad, and culminating senior experiences were strongly and positively associated with students' perceived gains in learning and development, and with engagement in deep approaches to learning (NSSE, 2007). Building on 10 years of research with NSSE, Kuh recommended that institutions provide opportunities for all students to participate in at least two high-impact activities in their undergraduate career, one in the first year and one after the first year (NSSE, 2007).

Of course, not all programs designed to make a difference in student success are necessarily "high-impact." Rather, high-impact practices are distinguished by six important characteristics (Kuh, 2008; NSSE, 2007). First, they require a substantial amount of time and effort directed toward a

NEW DIRECTIONS FOR INSTITUTIONAL RESEARCH, no. 160 ©2014 Wiley Periodicals, Inc.
Published online in Wiley Online Library (wileyonlinelibrary.com) • DOI: 10.1002/ir.20059

challenging educational goal. Second, high-impact practices are not typically pursued in isolation, but involve shared intellectual experiences with faculty and peers. Interactions with others who have shared interests provide more opportunities for personal and intellectual growth, and ultimately, student success. Third, students step outside of their routine environments and settings, and are exposed to a diversity of novel ideas, worldviews, and practices. Fourth, students in these activities generally receive frequent and continuous feedback about their performance, which is instrumental for growth and improvement. Programs that create conditions for frequent feedback help students stay engaged and focused on learning and achievement. Fifth, high-impact activities provide opportunities for students to apply what they learn in the classroom in different settings, experiencing firsthand how to approach real-world problems and situations. Finally, they create conditions conducive to deep learning, where students synthesize ideas and concepts that cumulatively make a noticeable change in students' worldviews and self-awareness.

Using data from the 2011 administration of NSSE, we focus on first-year students who participated in selected high-impact practices and examine the effects on deep learning, self-reported gains, and overall satisfaction with the first-year experience. While a number of high-impact practices were shown to bring positive effects for deep learning and overall engagement (Kuh, 2008), we limit our analysis to three gathered by NSSE for first-year students: service learning, learning communities, and undergraduate research.

Service Learning

Service learning is a pedagogical approach by which students participate in a structured community project as part of a regular course. Specifically, Bringle and Hatcher (1996) define service learning as:

> a credit-bearing educational experience in which students participate in an organized service activity that meets identified community needs and reflect on the service activity in such a way as to gain further understanding of the course content, a broader appreciation of the discipline, and an enhanced sense of civic responsibility. Unlike extracurricular voluntary service, service-learning is a course-based service experience that produces the best outcomes when meaningful service activities are related to course material through reflection activities such as directed writings, small group discussions, and class presentations. Unlike practica and internships, the experiential activity in a service-learning course is not necessarily skill-based within the context of professional education. (p. 222)

An important distinction of service learning from traditional community service is its purposefulness and academic rigor (Zlotkowski, 2005),

NEW DIRECTIONS FOR INSTITUTIONAL RESEARCH • DOI: 10.1002/ir

which contribute to the activity's "high-impact" description. Participating in a service-learning activity with other students and an instructor allows for shared intellectual experiences with faculty and peers, exposes one to the views of other individuals, and provides opportunities for frequent feedback. With facilitated reflection in the form of papers or group discussions, students become aware of their own worldviews, values, beliefs, and moral principles.

Service learning has found support in research on learning outcomes. For example, service learning was positively associated with growth in critical thinking, writing skills, GPA, and commitment to racial understanding and activism (Astin, Vogelgesang, Ikeda, & Yee, 2000). Other studies found that service learning contributed to higher retention (Gallini & Moely, 2003; Nigro & Farnsworth, 2009) and gains in promoting moral judgment (King & Mayhew, 2002). A comprehensive review found substantial evidence of the positive effects of service learning on student personal development (such as identity development, spiritual growth, moral development, and self-efficacy), interpersonal development, leadership and communication skills, promoting cultural and racial understanding, social responsibility and commitment to service, and academic learning, among many other outcomes (Eyler & Giles, 2001).

However, service learning must be conducted with sensitivity to the needs and understandings of first-year students. First-year students find themselves in a vulnerable and transitional position, and so the service-learning activity should be carefully designed to align and expand their capabilities (Zlotkowski, 2005).

Using NSSE Data: Augustana College (IL). Augustana College used NSSE results to support several goals of its 2005 strategic plan, prepared as part of the college's self-study for Higher Learning Commission reaccreditation. Among the plan's six broad goals, NSSE scores showed that Augustana students were more likely than students attending peer institutions to participate in volunteerism and community service, but many did not do so as part of regular coursework. Over the next few years, the Center for Vocational Reflection at Augustana took the lead on initiatives to shift the focus from service alone to service, engagement, and learning through existing programs such as learning communities. They drew on resources and support of the Illinois Campus Compact, a coalition of campuses that foster campus–community programs, to help faculty integrate service learning into their courses. Within two years, service-learning participation by students had increased by 6% and by 2012 the participation rates had become substantially larger.

Learning Communities

While learning communities are present in many forms from one campus to the next, in general they are groups of students who take a number of classes together, often connected by an interdisciplinary theme, and participate as a group in cocurricular and extracurricular activities (Matthews, Smith, MacGregor, & Gabelnick, 1997). Specifically, Laufgraben (2005) defined learning communities as:

> clusters of courses organized around a curricular theme [that] students take as a group and that strengthen and enrich students' connection to each other, their teachers, and the subject matter they are studying. They also challenge first-year students to redefine their educational goals in broader terms and provide the support for doing so. (p. 371)

Learning communities are identified by five dimensions that fit nicely with their classification as a high-impact practice: student collaboration, faculty collaboration, curricular coordination, shared setting, and intensive pedagogy (Love & Tokuno, 1999). Several studies have found numerous positive outcomes for students participating in learning communities, such as achievement, retention, intellectual and social development, increased interaction with faculty, and greater participation in academic and cocurricular activities (Laufgraben, 2005).

Living-learning programs are a specific type of learning community "that involve undergraduate students who live together in a discrete portion of a residence hall (or the entire hall); have staff and resources dedicated for that program only; and participants partake in special academic and/or extracurricular programming designed especially for them" (Kurotsuchi Inkelas, 2010, p. 4). However, the benefits of such programs for first-year students appear to vary. For example, students in the living-learning programs at the University of Michigan interacted more with faculty and engaged in more discussions of sociocultural issues with their peers. These effects, in turn, influenced students' career goals and their intellectual and personal growth. The students also received better grades and exhibited higher levels of intellectual curiosity (Kurotsuchi Inkelas, 2000). Living-learning programs were also associated with helping students make smoother academic and social transitions and a better sense of belonging. However, living-learning programs did not associate with gains in critical thinking, diversity appreciation, a sense of civic engagement, application of knowledge abilities, and growth in cognitive complexity (Kurotsuchi Inkelas, 2010). Thus, living-learning programs were found to be limited in promoting learning outcomes but helpful with college transition for first-year students. Kurotsuchi Inkelas (2010) noted that many of the surveyed programs lacked one or more of the essential structural, academic, or cocurricular components of an effective living-learning experience, which may explain some of the low or moderate effects.

Using NSSE Data: Indiana University Purdue University-Indianapolis (IUPUI; IN). IUPUI annually monitors trends over time and the impact of programmatic interventions by using NSSE one year and its own ongoing student survey the next. After finding few differences in first-year student persistence between those in "regular" learning communities (linked classes) and those enrolled in thematic learning communities (when faculty work together across sections to infuse interdisciplinary learning), University College staff speculated that being part of a cohort experience is itself enough to enhance student persistence. This appears to be especially the case for students admitted conditionally. However, NSSE data show that students in the thematic learning communities were more engaged compared with other students. Based on NSSE data and other academic success indicators (GPAs and retention rates), IUPUI's themed learning community program was expanded and resulted in an increase in first-year participation from 36% in 2006 to 47% in 2009.

Undergraduate Research

Undergraduate research is "an inquiry or investigation conducted by an undergraduate student that makes an original intellectual or creative contribution to the discipline" (Council on Undergraduate Research, n.d., para. 3), and includes scientific inquiry, creative activity, and scholarship (Kinkead, 2003). Others emphasized the collaborative nature of the activity between a faculty mentor and a promising scholar or group of scholars (National Conferences on Undergraduate Research, n.d.). In these activities, students learn about current work in the discipline, develop skills and techniques, undertake research and inquiry, and engage in scholarly discussion (Healy & Jenkins, 2009). Unlike other high-impact practices that are characterized by highly recognizable and observable features, structures, and organization, the elements of undergraduate research are an expansion of what is already done within individual course assignments. In fact, many institutions have built research activities into their formal curricula because of the recognized value of the activity. That is why the updated version of NSSE dropped the stipulation that the activity must be done "outside of course or program requirements," and merely asks students if they have done "work with a faculty member on a research project" (NSSE, 2013, p. 2).

Undergraduate research is associated with many professional, academic, cognitive, and personal benefits. For example, students who participated in an undergraduate research experience improved their research potential in areas such as general knowledge and understanding of science, data collection, designing a study, lab techniques, interpreting results, and independent thinking (Bauer & Bennett, 2003; Kardash, 2000; Lopatto, 2004; Mabrouk & Peters, 2000; Seymour, Hunter, Laursen, & DeAntoni, 2004). Importantly, self-ratings were validated by the students' faculty research mentors (Kardash, 2000). Undergraduate research was also linked to gains in personal development, such as overcoming obstacles, working independently, and professional self-confidence (Bauer & Bennett, 2003;

Hunter, Laursen, & Seymour, 2007; Lopatto, 2004; Mabrouk & Peters, 2000; Seymour et al., 2004), as well as the development of professional identity (Hunter et al., 2007). Other gains included developing professional collegiality with faculty mentors and peers, refinement of career and post-graduation plans (Seymour et al., 2004), and improved communication skills within the research context (Bauer & Bennett, 2003; Kardash, 2000; Seymour et al., 2004). Alumni who participated in undergraduate research noted more overall satisfaction and growth within their undergraduate careers (Bauer & Bennett, 2003). Finally, the University of Michigan Undergraduate Research Opportunity Program (University of Michigan, 2012) specifically targeted first-year and sophomore students and was linked to improved sophomore retention (Nagda, Gregerman, Jonides, Von Hippel, & Lerner, 1998). This finding may suggest that the benefits of first-year research—consistent with all high-impact practices—may be delayed or cumulative rather than immediate.

Conducting research with faculty may be beneficial, but is uncommon among first-year students who need time to get exposed to various disciplines, interact with different faculty members, and explore their academic interests. While the precise number of first-year students engaged in undergraduate research is unknown, NSSE estimated the proportion to be only about one in twenty students (NSSE, 2011). In fact, even among a prescreened sample of first-year students who already possessed personal and academic inclinations toward advanced degrees in health and behavioral sciences majors, the proportion involved in research with faculty was only 12% (Hurtado et al., 2008). Undergraduate research programs in the United States were more likely to exist in research universities and small liberal arts colleges, and were more prevalent in the sciences (Healy & Jenkins, 2009; NSSE, 2011), but while these differences were evident in senior participation rates, they were not observable for first-year students (NSSE, 2011).

Using NSSE Data: Clemson University (SC). In 2006, Clemson University initiated their Creative Inquiry Projects—undergraduate research activities where faculty members guide small groups of students through a multisemester project in various disciplines. Projects were designed to help students develop problem-solving and critical thinking skills, as well as the abilities to work on teams and express themselves effectively in written and verbal communication. "Research is important at Clemson, but not just with faculty and graduate students. Before graduating nearly every undergraduate student has the opportunity to participate in a creative inquiry or other research project" (Clemson University, 2008, para. 2). According to Clemson's NSSE results, the number of students participating in undergraduate research is significantly higher than at institutions in Clemson's selected peer group.

NEW DIRECTIONS FOR INSTITUTIONAL RESEARCH • DOI: 10.1002/ir

Methods

This section describes the data and measures that were used for this study and how the analyses were performed.

Sample. The data for this study came from the 2011 administration of NSSE and include nearly 140,000 first-year student respondents enrolled at 562 U.S. institutions. Fifty-four percent of respondents were female and 95% were enrolled full time. About half (48%) of the first-year students in the sample were enrolled in doctorate-granting institutions, 38% at master's colleges and universities, and 13% at baccalaureate colleges. Most of the students in the sample (74%) were enrolled in public institutions. The data were weighted to preserve the sample proportions of male and female students, full-time and part-time students, and institutional proportions within the total first-year student population of the participating institutions.

Measures. Dependent variables included three subscales that gauge the extent to which students practiced deep approaches to learning, three scales which captured students' estimates of their own growth and development, and one overall satisfaction scale.

Deep Approaches to Learning. High-impact practices, when done well, promote and facilitate deep approaches to learning (NSSE, 2007). *Deep learning*, as opposed to *surface learning* (Marton & Säljö, 1976), results from an intention of a learner to understand the material, while surface learning is associated with other goals, such as to pass an exam, receive a grade, and so on (Nelson Laird, Shoup, & Kuh, 2006). NSSE contains a short set of items that measures three distinctive aspects of deep learning: higher order learning, integrative learning, and reflective learning (Nelson Laird et al., 2006; see Appendix). The *higher order learning* subscale investigates how much the student's courses emphasized advanced thinking skills such as analysis, synthesis, evaluation, and application of course material to real situations. The *integrative learning* subscale gauges the student's exposure to diverse ideas and perspectives, as well as the ability to integrate these views. The *reflective learning* subscale asks students how often they reflected on their own views and understanding. The three subscales were found to correlate with one another sufficiently to conclude that they were all manifestations of a single deep learning factor (Nelson Laird, Shoup, Kuh, & Schwartz, 2008).

Self-Reported Gains. Three NSSE scales that measure self-reported outcomes, or gains, ask students to estimate the amount of progress they have made in an array of learning outcomes. These include gains in personal and social development, gains in practical competencies, and gains in general education learning (see Appendix). Gains in personal and social development cover the student's progress in self-understanding, values clarification, independent learning, civic awareness, and spirituality. Gains in practical competencies involve making progress in career skills, working with others, using computers and technology, analyzing quantitative problems, and solving real-world problems. Finally, gains in general education deal with the student's sense of becoming a better writer, speaker, and critical thinker as a result of his or her college experience. Self-reported gains are more correctly interpreted as measures of student attitudes about their learning, and not as measures of direct learning outcomes, but still hold merit for institutional assessment (Gonyea & Miller, 2011).

Satisfaction With the First-Year Experience. Finally, the NSSE survey asks two questions about how satisfied students are with their college experience. One asks students about general satisfaction with the institution, and the other asks if they would choose the same institution again, had they been able to start over (see Appendix).

Analysis. To begin our analysis we examined the demographic composition of the first-year students who participated in learning communities, service learning, and undergraduate research, as well as the characteristics of institutions where those experiences took place. Then, to estimate the magnitude of the relationship between participation in each high-impact practice and our dependent measures, we ran 21 simple ordinary least squares regression models where each of the seven dependent variables was regressed on a common set of student and institutional characteristics, plus one of the three high-impact practice measures. Student characteristics included gender, enrollment status (full-time vs. part-time), ethnicity, living arrangement (on campus or off campus), international status, age, major, self-reported grades, and first-generation status. Institutional characteristics included enrollment size, control (public or private), and selectivity as reported in Barron's (2009) *Profiles of American Colleges.* Controlling for these characteristics allowed us to attain a closer estimate of the net effect each of the three high-impact practices has on deep approaches to learning, self-reported gains, and satisfaction.

Results. The following results examine the relationship between participation in each high-impact practice and our dependent measures.

Student Characteristics. Table 2.1 shows the prevalence of first-year participation in the three high-impact practices by student characteristics. The most common of the three was service learning with 40% of first-year students having done it at least "sometimes" during the first year. Less common were learning communities, where less than one in five (18%) first-year students participated, and undergraduate research with only about one in twenty (5%) first-year students in the sample. There were no gender differences among students who participated in these three activities, but Black and Hispanic students participated in all three practices at slightly higher rates than students of other ethnic groups, including Whites. Full-time students, understandably, participated at much higher levels than did part-time students in service learning (41%/30%) and learning communities (19%/12%) but no such differences were evident among the small portion of students who did research with faculty. Interestingly, international students participated more often

Table 2.1. Participation in Service Learning, Learning Communities, and Research With Faculty by First-Year Student Characteristics

Student Characteristics		Service Learning		Learning Community		Research With Faculty	
		N	%	N	%	N	%
Gender	Female	24,156	40	9,438	15	3,360	5
	Male	32,033	42	13,309	17	3,911	5
Race/ethnicity	African American	5,699	45	2,738	22	870	7
	American Indian/Alaska Native	286	39	134	18	44	6
	Asian/Pacific Islander	3,300	42	1,351	17	375	5
	Caucasian/White	30,504	39	14,887	19	3,390	4
	Hispanic	4,418	40	2,147	19	542	5
Enrollment	Full-time	53,330	41	25,209	19	6,315	5
	Part-time	1,784	30	701	12	340	6
International	International	4,118	52	1,299	16	653	8
	United States	50,644	40	24,480	19	5,955	5
First-generation*	First-generation	22,312	40	9,763	18	2,807	5
	Not first-generation	31,954	40	15,796	20	3,729	5
Transfer	Transfer	3,772	35	1,635	15	6,049	5
	Native	51,178	41	24,214	19	6,049	5
Age	Adult (at least 25)	2,078	27	964	12	442	6
	Traditional (under 25)	52,942	41	24,917	19	6,198	5
Major category	Arts and humanities	5,676	36	3,021	19	633	4
	Biological sciences	5,365	41	2,584	20	809	6
	Business	7,369	42	3,202	18	851	5
	Education	5,034	50	2,056	20	464	5
	Engineering	4,545	36	2,897	23	624	5
	Physical sciences	2,047	37	987	18	375	7
	Other professional	6,782	42	3,219	20	716	4
	Social sciences	6,366	40	2,933	18	733	5

*Neither parent had earned a baccalaureate degree.

than domestic students in service learning (52%/40%) and research with faculty (8%/5%). Encouragingly, first-generation students participated as often as their peers in all three practices. Older first-year students (at least 25 years of age) and first-year transfer students were less likely to engage in service learning and learning communities, but were on par with their counterparts in research. The breakdown of students' majors and expected majors revealed no considerable differences with one exception—education majors engaged more in service learning than all other major field categories.

Institutional Characteristics.   Descriptive results showing the prevalence of high-impact practices among first-year students by institutional characteristics are shown in Table 2.2. First-year students enrolled in doctorate-granting universities and at larger institutions in general were more involved in learning communities than were students at other types of institutions. On the other hand, students enrolled in smaller, bachelor's-granting institutions participated more in service learning. Neither Carnegie type nor enrollment size appears to affect the frequency of first-year students doing research with faculty. With regard to institutional control, first-year students attending private colleges and universities were more involved in service learning than their counterparts at public schools, and students at more competitive schools participated more often in learning communities.

Regression Analyses.   After controlling for student and institutional characteristics, the relationships between each of the three high-impact practices and each dependent variable were statistically significant (Table 2.3). The magnitude of these relationships, however, varied across dependent and independent variables, ranging from small to moderate.

Of the three high-impact practices, service learning had the strongest associations with all seven outcomes. Service learning contributed substantially to integrative learning and to personal and social gains, with smaller effects on higher order learning, reflective learning, practical gains, and gains in general education. This is consistent with previous research which concluded that participation in service learning or community projects brings numerous positive benefits to students' cognitive and personal growth as well as students' ability to apply what they learned in "the real world" (Eyler & Giles, 2001). Learning communities had generally small effects but were more associated with integrative learning and reflective learning than other dependent measures. Research with faculty had generally small effects as well but more substantial effects were observed for integrative learning and personal and social gains.

Conclusions

It appears that a first-year student is more likely to participate in service learning at smaller, private institutions. Many such institutions espouse community service, civic engagement, and moral or religious education as

NEW DIRECTIONS FOR INSTITUTIONAL RESEARCH • DOI: 10.1002/ir

Table 2.2. First-Year Participation in Service Learning, Learning Communities, and Research With Faculty, by Institution Characteristics

Institution Characteristics		Service Learning		Learning Community		Research With Faculty	
		N	%	N	%	N	%
Carnegie Classification	Doctoral Research University—very high research activity	11,258	36	6,909	22	1,499	5
	Doctoral Research University—high research activity	10,142	41	5,969	24	1,189	5
	Doctoral Research University	4,245	44	1,856	19	541	6
	Universities with master's programs—large	15,574	40	6,419	16	1,812	5
	Universities with master's programs—medium	4,268	43	1,567	16	485	5
	Universities with master's programs—small	1,658	44	620	16	201	5
	Baccalaureate colleges—arts and sciences	3,881	42	1,210	13	415	4
	Baccalaureate colleges—diverse fields	3,867	46	1,262	15	486	6
Enrollment size	Up to 500	108	55	27	14	14	7
	501–1,000	1,102	50	327	15	139	6
	1,001–2,000	4,974	50	1,581	16	537	5
	2,001–3,000	5,178	47	1,680	15	500	5
	3,001–5,000	5,433	43	2,108	17	628	5
	5,001–10,000	9,629	39	4,146	17	1,240	5
	10,001–20,000	13,954	38	6,405	18	1,662	5
	More than 20,000	14,736	37	9,637	24	1,936	5
Control	Public	37,295	37	19,265	19	4,875	5
	Private	17,780	50	6,629	18	1,770	5
Selectivity (Barron's)	Noncompetitive	2,687	37	1,273	18	456	6
	Less competitive	4,742	40	1,941	16	674	6
	Competitive	25,897	41	11,899	19	3,196	5
	Very competitive	14,548	43	7,262	21	1,491	5
	Highly competitive	6,061	36	3,228	19	703	4
	Most competitive	1,179	32	305	8	134	4

Table 2.3. Relationships[a] Between High-Impact Practices and Selected Outcomes in the First Year of College

Dependent Variables[b]		Service Learning	Learning Community	Research With Faculty
Deep approaches to learning	Higher order learning	++	+	+
	Integrative learning	+++	++	++
	Reflective learning	++	++	+
Self-reported gains	Practical	++	+	+
	Personal and social	+++	+	++
	General education	++	+	+
Satisfaction with the first-year experience		+	+	+

[a]Key: $+p < .001$, $++p < .001$ and standardized beta $> .1$, and $+++p < .001$ and standardized beta $> .2$.
[b]Student level controls included gender, enrollment (part-time or full-time), race or ethnicity, international status, age, major, self-reported grades, and first-generation status. Institution-level controls included enrollment size, control (public or private), and Barron's selectivity index.

part of their mission, and therefore establish courses with a service-learning component. In turn, of the three high-impact practices we examined, service learning holds the strongest relationships with deep approaches to learning, self-reported gains, and student satisfaction. It may be that the effects of service learning are more immediate and proximal to other forms of engagement and to students' attitudes toward learning, unlike other high-impact practices which accumulate over time. Engagement in service learning often requires students to evaluate their experiences through journaling, reflective writing, facilitated discussions, and/or other thoughtful activities which—when done well—promote awareness of the connections between the service activity and the student's coursework, academic and career interests, and overall connectedness to the institution.

Learning community programs are more common at larger institutions, most likely because of a desire to create smaller, personal, and more navigable environments for first-year students. In addition, larger institutions have more resources to establish an array of specialized and thematic program offerings that are able to meet the diverse needs of first-year students. On the other hand, students at small institutions often experience the entire incoming cohort as a "learning community" where they sit in the same courses, live in the same buildings, and learn from the same faculty. In this light, it is not surprising that learning communities would be more operative on large campuses. Yet, the effect of learning communities is modest for first-year students. More needs to be learned about the characteristics and components of the learning community programs that are offered from one institution to the next. What works for large universities may not be effective at small colleges. It is also possible that learning community programs have cumulative effects which do not become apparent until later in the student's undergraduate career.

Of the three high-impact practices examined in this chapter, undergraduate research is the least utilized by first-year students and the least discriminating among student and institutional types. Several factors are needed for first-year students to be involved in research, such as a personal dispositions toward research, including self-efficacy and goal commitment; support of peer networks and institutional agents; and institutional structures (Hurtado et al., 2008). Notably, international students participated in research at a significantly higher rate (8%) than domestic students (5%). This may be partially explained by the inclination of international students to major in STEM disciplines (Zhao, Kuh, & Carini, 2005) which provide more opportunities for research.

The effects of the three high-impact practices on deep approaches to learning, self-reported gains, and satisfaction with the first-year experience ranged from small to moderate. This should be taken as a cautionary tale, for simply organizing an activity that resembles a high-impact practice does not guarantee strong results and learning gains. For a high-impact practice to actually have high impact it should be implemented well with a vision of a purpose, which clearly requires deliberate planning and effort on behalf of the institution, administrative and academic staff.

Still, service learning, learning communities, and undergraduate research are considered "high-impact" because they have measurable positive effects, as demonstrated in this chapter. These effects are produced for good reason. Each of these activities requires extended time and energy beyond a typical first-year student's schedule. They put students in real situations where they must engage and grapple with problems collaboratively and with caring advisors and faculty. They guide students out of their comfort zones and help them interact with diverse others on campus, in the community, and in new settings which are, at first, unfamiliar. Faculty and advisors provide continuous and detailed feedback on their performance. And finally, these activities create the conditions for deep learning by asking students to reflect on their understandings, reconcile new ideas with old ones, and integrate learning from one setting to be useful in other settings. High-impact activities may only represent one facet of a student's undergraduate career, but if implemented well, the student will reap cumulative benefits in the first year and beyond. Providing the opportunity for all new students to participate in at least one high-impact practice in the first year will bring positive results in student learning and development.

References

Astin, A. W., Vogelgesang, L. J., Ikeda, E. K., & Yee, J. A. (2000). *How service learning affects students*. Retrieved from http://heri.ucla.edu/PDFs/HSLAS/HSLAS.PDF

Barron's. (2009). *2009 Barron's profiles of American colleges* (28th ed.). Hauppauge, NY: Barron's Educational Series.

Bauer, K. W., & Bennett, J. S. (2003). Alumni perceptions used to assess the undergraduate research experience. *Journal of Higher Education, 74*(2), 210–230.

Bringle, R. G., & Hatcher, J. A. (1996). Implementing service-learning in higher education. *Journal of Higher Education, 67*(2), 221–239.

Clemson University. (2008). *Clemson students engaged in learning.* Retrieved from http://www.clemson.edu/academics/nsse/index.html

Council on Undergraduate Research. (n.d.). *About CUR.* Retrieved from http://www.cur.org/about.html

Eyler, J., & Giles, D. (2001). *At a glance: What we know about the effects of service-learning on college students, faculty, institutions, and communities, 1993–2000: Third Edition.* New York, NY: Corporation for National and Community Service.

Gallini, S. M., & Moely, B. E. (2003). Service-learning and engagement, academic challenge, and retention. *Michigan Journal of Community Service Learning, 10*(1), 5–14.

Gonyea, R. M., & Miller, A. (2011). Clearing the AIR about the use of self-reported gains in institutional research. In S. Herzog & N. A. Bowman (Eds.), *New Directions for Institutional Research: No. 150. Validity and limitations of college student self-reported data* (pp. 99–111). San Francisco, CA: Jossey-Bass.

Healy, M., & Jenkins, A. (2009). *Developing undergraduate research and inquiry.* York, UK: HE Academy.

Hunter, A.-B., Laursen, S., & Seymour, E. (2007). Becoming a scientist: The role of undergraduate research in students' cognitive, personal and professional development. *Science Education, 91*(1), 36–74.

Hurtado, S., Eagan, M. K., Cabrera, N. L., Lin, M. H., Park, J., & Lopez, M. (2008). Training future scientists: Predicting first-year minority student participation in health science research. *Research in Higher Education, 49*(2), 126–152.

Kardash, C. M. (2000). Evaluation of an undergraduate research experience: Perceptions of undergraduate interns and their faculty mentors. *Journal of Educational Psychology, 92*(1), 191–201.

King, P. M., & Mayhew, M. J. (2002). Moral judgment development in higher education: Insights from the Defining Issues Test. *Journal of Moral Education, 31*(3), 247–270.

Kinkead, J. (2003). Learning through inquiry: An overview of undergraduate research. In J. Kinkead (Ed.), *New Directions for Teaching and Learning: No. 93. Valuing and supporting undergraduate research* (pp. 5–18). San Francisco, CA: Jossey-Bass.

Kuh, G. D. (2008). *High-impact educational practices: What they are, who has access to them, and why they matter.* Washington, DC: Association of American Colleges and Universities.

Kurotsuchi Inkelas, K. (2000). *Participation in living-learning programs at the University of Michigan: Benefits for students and faculty* (Occasional CRLT Paper no. 15). Ann Arbor: Center for Research on Learning and Teaching, University of Michigan. Retrieved from http://www.crlt.umich.edu/publinks/CRLT_no15.pdf

Kurotsuchi Inkelas, K. (2010, February). *Lessons learned about one high-impact practice.* Program presented at the annual conference on the First Year Experience, Denver, CO.

Laufgraben, J. L. (2005). Learning communities. In M. L. Upcraft, J. N. Gardner, B. O. Barefoot, & Associates (Eds.), *Challenging and supporting the first-year student: A handbook for improving the first year of college* (pp. 371–387). San Francisco, CA: Jossey-Bass.

Lopatto, D. (2004). Survey of undergraduate research experiences (SURE): First findings. *Cell Biology Education, 3*(4), 270–277.

Love G. A., & Tokuno, K. (1999). Learning community models. In J. H. Levine (Ed.), *Learning communities: New structures, new partnerships for learning* (pp. 9–18).

Columbia, SC: National Resource Center for the First-Year Experience and Students in Transition.

Mabrouk, P. A., & Peters, K. (2000, April 3–May 5). *Student perspectives on undergraduate research (UR) experiences in chemistry and biology.* Paper presented at The Role and Nature of Research by Undergraduates in Chemistry (Online conference). Retrieved from http://confchem.ccce.us/sites/default/files/2000SpringConfChemP2.pdf

Marton, F., & Säljö, R. (1976). On qualitative differences in learning. I: Outcome and process. *British Journal of Educational Psychology, 46*(1), 4–11.

Matthews, R. S., Smith, B. L., MacGregor, J., & Gabelnick, F. (1997). Creating learning communities. In J. G. Gaff & J. I. Ratcliff (Eds.), *Handbook of the undergraduate curriculum: A comprehensive guide to purposes, structures, practices, and change* (pp. 457–475). San Francisco, CA: Jossey-Bass.

Nagda, B. A., Gregerman, S. R., Jonides, J., Von Hippel, W., & Lerner, J. S. (1998). Undergraduate student-faculty research partnerships affect student retention. *Review of Higher Education, 22*(1), 55–72.

National Conferences on Undergraduate Research. (n.d.). *Undergraduate research.* Retrieved from http://www.ncur.org/ugresearch.htm

National Survey of Student Engagement (NSSE). (2007). *Experiences that matter: Enhancing student learning and success.* Bloomington: Center for Postsecondary Research, Indiana University.

National Survey of Student Engagement (NSSE). (2011). *Summary tables.* Retrieved from http://nsse.iub.edu/html/summary_tables.cfm

National Survey of Student Engagement (NSSE). (2013). *NSSE survey instrument.* Retrieved from http://nsse.iub.edu/pdf/survey_instruments/2013/2013%20NSSE%20Instrument.pdf

Nelson Laird, T. F., Shoup, R., & Kuh, G. D. (2006, May). *Measuring deep approaches to learning using the National Survey of Student Engagement.* Paper presented at the Annual Forum of the Association of Institutional Research, Chicago, IL.

Nelson Laird, T. F., Shoup, R., Kuh, G. D., & Schwartz, M. J. (2008). The effects of discipline on deep approaches to student learning and college outcomes. *Research in Higher Education, 49*(6), 469–494.

Nigro, G., & Farnsworth, N. (2009). *The effects of service-learning on retention.* Retrieved from http://www.compact.org/wp-content/uploads/2009/08/09-necc-sl-and-retention-report-for-webdoc.pdf

Seymour, E., Hunter, A., Laursen, S., & DeAntoni, T. (2004). Establishing the benefits of research experiences for undergraduates: First findings from a three-year study. *Science Education, 88*(4), 493–534.

University of Michigan. (2012). *Undergraduate Research Opportunity Program.* Retrieved from http://www.lsa.umich.edu/urop/

Zhao, C.-M., Kuh, G. D., & Carini, R. M. (2005). A comparison of international student and American student engagement in effective educational practices. *The Journal of Higher Education, 76*(2), 209–231.

Zlotkowski, E. (2005). Service-learning and the first-year student. In M. L. Upcraft, J. N. Gardner, & B. O. Barefoot (Eds.), *The freshman year experience: Helping students survive and succeed in college* (pp. 356–370). San Francisco, CA: Jossey-Bass.

MALIKA TUKIBAYEVA is a PhD student in higher education and student affairs at Indiana University Bloomington.

ROBERT M. GONYEA is an associate director of the Indiana University Center for Postsecondary Research.

NEW DIRECTIONS FOR INSTITUTIONAL RESEARCH • DOI: 10.1002/ir

Appendix: Dependent Variables: Scales and Component Items
Approaches to Deep Learning

Higher Order Learning.   During the current school year, how much has your coursework emphasized the following mental activities?

* Analyzing the basic elements of an idea, experience, or theory, such as examining a particular case or situation in depth and considering its components.
* Synthesizing and organizing ideas, information, or experiences into new, more complex interpretations and relationships.
* Making judgments about the value of information, arguments, or methods, such as examining how others gathered and interpreted data and assessing the soundness of their conclusions.
* Applying theories or concepts to practical problems or in new situations.

Integrative Learning.   In your experience at your institution during the current school year, about how often have you done each of the following?

* Worked on a paper or project that required integrating ideas or information from various sources.
* Included diverse perspectives (different races, religions, genders, political beliefs, etc.) in class discussions or writing assignments.
* Put together ideas or concepts from different courses when completing assignments or during class.
* Discussed ideas from your readings or classes with faculty members outside of class.
* Discussed ideas from your readings or classes with others outside of class (students, family members, coworkers, etc.).

Reflective Learning.   During the current school year, about how often have you done each of the following?

* Examined the strengths and weaknesses of your own views on a topic or issue.
* Tried to better understand someone else's views by imagining how an issue looks from his or her.
* Learned something that changed the way you understand an issue or concept.

Self-Reported Gains

Practical Gains. To what extent has your experience at this institution contributed to your knowledge, skills, and personal development in the following areas?

- Acquiring job or work-related knowledge and skills.
- Working effectively with others.
- Using computing and information technology.
- Analyzing quantitative problems.
- Solving complex real-world problems.

Personal and Social Gains. To what extent has your experience at this institution contributed to your knowledge, skills, and personal development in the following areas?

- Developing a personal code of values and ethics.
- Understanding yourself.
- Understanding people of other racial and ethnic backgrounds.
- Voting in local, state (provincial), or national (federal) elections.
- Learning effectively on your own.
- Contributing to the welfare of your community.
- Developing a deepened sense of spirituality.

General Education Gains. To what extent has your experience at this institution contributed to your knowledge, skills, and personal development in the following areas?

- Writing clearly and effectively.
- Speaking clearly and effectively.
- Acquiring a broad general education.
- Thinking critically and analytically.

Student Satisfaction

- How would you evaluate your entire educational experience at this institution?
- If you could start over again, would you go to the same institution you are now attending?

3

This chapter demonstrates that the effects of good teaching and academic challenge on leadership and psychological well-being during the first year of college differ for African-American and White students, which suggests that institutional researchers should disaggregate data by race or other relevant student characteristics when trying to understand the relationship between experiences and outcomes for first-year students.

Good Practices for Whom? A Vital Question for Understanding the First Year of College

Kathleen M. Goodman

"Good teaching" and "academic challenge" are two aspects of teaching and learning that have become associated with a fairly well-known list of good practices in undergraduate education (Blimling, Whitt, & Associates, 1999; Chickering & Gamson, 1987, 1991, 1999; Kuh, Kinzie, Schuh, Whitt, & Associates, 2005; Pascarella, 2008). Good practices consist of behaviors and conditions that promote student learning and development such as active learning, student–faculty contact, prompt feedback, positive peer interactions, supportive environments, clear communications, and high expectations (Blimling et al., 1999; Chickering & Gamson, 1987, 1991, 1999; Kuh et al., 2005; Pascarella, 2008). The College Student Experiences Questionnaire, the National Study of Student Engagement (NSSE), and the Wabash National Study of Liberal Arts Education (Wabash National Study)—national studies that institutions of higher education use to guide their work—have questions to measure the extent to which students experience good practices and the relationship of those practices to educational outcomes (Chickering & Gamson, 1999; Kuh et al., 2005; Pascarella, 2008; Pascarella, Wolniak, Cruce, & Blaich, 2004).

Analyses of 19 institutions in the quantitative portion of the Wabash National Study demonstrated that, in the first year of college, good

This research was supported by a generous grant from the Center of Inquiry in the Liberal Arts at Wabash College to the Center for Research on Undergraduate Education at The University of Iowa.

NEW DIRECTIONS FOR INSTITUTIONAL RESEARCH, no. 160 © 2014 Wiley Periodicals, Inc.
Published online in Wiley Online Library (wileyonlinelibrary.com) • DOI: 10.1002/ir.20060

teaching and academic challenge positively affect many of the outcomes associated with liberal arts education, including development of socially responsible leadership, psychological well-being, intercultural effectiveness, and inclination to inquire (Seifert, Goodman, King, & Baxter Magolda, 2010). Furthermore, qualitative interviews of 315 students at six of those institutions identified challenging courses and transition to college intellectual and community life as meaningful (Seifert et al., 2010). When students spoke of the transition to college, they mentioned first-year seminars, engaging courses, and learning how to actively participate in discussions, most of which align with good teaching practices (Seifert et al., 2010).

Given the prevalence of research demonstrating the benefit of good practices, and the specific evidence about good teaching and academic challenge, an analysis of conditional effects of good practices on liberal arts outcomes during the first year of college using the Wabash National Study provided some surprising results. The study found that for African-American students, compared to White students, academic challenge provided an extra gain in six of the 30 outcomes studied (Goodman, 2010). However, it also found that for African-American students, compared to White students, good teaching provided less of a benefit on 11 of the 30 outcomes studied (Goodman, 2010). Most of those differences were related to personal and interpersonal growth in areas of leadership and psychological well-being. The findings of that report suggest that good practices in general, and good teaching and academic challenge in particular, may not influence all students in the same way. This is consistent with prior research that demonstrates that students of different racial backgrounds experience college in different ways (Hurtado, Milem, Clayton-Pedersen, & Allen, 1998).

The purpose of this study is to further analyze the relationship between good teaching and academic challenge on leadership and psychological well-being outcomes during the first year of college for African-American and White students. I begin with an extension of the analysis used in the Goodman (2010) report by analyzing two separate samples of students—African American and White. Then, in a second analysis, I break the good teaching and academic challenge scales into composite parts in an attempt to gain an understanding of the specific aspects of good teaching and academic challenge that differ in the influence on leadership and psychological well-being outcomes for African-American and White students. The specific research questions guiding the study are: (a) To what extent do the effects of good teaching and academic challenge on leadership and psychological well-being outcomes differ for African-American and White students in the first year of college? (b) What aspects of good teaching and academic challenge affect leadership and psychological well-being outcomes differently for African-American and White students in the first year of college?

New Directions for Institutional Research • DOI: 10.1002/ir

Methods

The data for this analysis come from the Wabash National Study, a mixed methods study designed to investigate the relationship between practices and conditions in undergraduate education and college outcomes associated with liberal arts education. The quantitative data, which is the focus of this study, were gathered from three different cohorts of students beginning their first year of college in 2006, 2007, and 2008. The students were first-time, full-time students. The institutions were both public and private and ranged from open admissions to highly selective. For the purposes of this analysis, I have limited the data to four-year institutions. Therefore, the students in the data are enrolled at 32 liberal arts colleges, nine regional institutions, and seven research universities in various geographic regions of the United States. I have divided the sample into two groups: White students ($N = 5,846$) and African-American students ($N = 764$).

Instruments and Data Collection. At the beginning of their first year of college, students in the Wabash National Study filled out surveys designed to collect data about their demographic background, high school experiences, and attitudes about college. These data provided controls to account for students' varying backgrounds. Students also took pretests designed to measure six different outcomes associated with liberal arts education, including (but not limited to) leadership and psychological well-being. The data from the first collection provide a baseline for understanding students' current leadership skills and psychological well-being as they entered college.

Toward the end of the first year of college, the same students were asked to fill out another battery of surveys. First, they provided information regarding the experiences they had, and the conditions they encountered, during the first year of college. Then they took posttest surveys (the same instruments that were used at the beginning of the year) representing liberal arts outcomes. Because they took a pretest and posttest assessment of each outcome, the analyses represent net changes during the first year of college.

Independent Variables. In each analysis in this study, I controlled for gender, low family income, first-generation status, high school ACT score, a scale representing academic motivation, and the number of liberal arts courses taken. I also controlled for institutional type (regional or research vs. liberal arts) and cohort (2007 or 2008 vs. 2006). I used these variables in an attempt to account for possible confounding influences on college experiences and outcomes. I also included the pretest score for each outcome, which is a control for past experiences and attitudes and provided a way to analyze net gains (or losses) on the outcomes.

The independent variables in the first stage of analyses are "megascales" representing good practices in undergraduate education: Good Teaching and Academic Challenge (the variables of interest) and Positive Peer

NEW DIRECTIONS FOR INSTITUTIONAL RESEARCH • DOI: 10.1002/ir

Interactions and Diverse Experiences, which serve as additional controls for college experiences. These scales were derived from a principal components analysis of the individual questions related to practices, experiences, and conditions encountered.

The Positive Peer Interactions megascale encompasses two smaller scales and nine questions. The individual questions ascertain the extent to which the student feels they have developed close personal relationships with other students at the institution. The scale has a Cronbach alpha of 0.85. The Diverse Experiences megascale encompasses two smaller scales and nine questions. The individual questions ascertain whether the student: developed relationships with students from a different racial background; participated in racial/cultural workshops; discussed religious, political, or personal differences with other students; and so on. The Cronbach alpha of the scale is 0.80.

The Good Teaching megascale encompasses four smaller scales and 23 questions representing Faculty Interest in Students, Prompt Academic Feedback, Positive Nonclassroom Interactions with Faculty, and Teaching Clarity. Table 3.1 shows the individual questions that comprise each subscale and the megascale. The Academic Challenge megascale encompasses four smaller scales and 31 questions representing Student's Academic Effort, Higher Order Thinking, Classes Challenge Thinking, and Integrative Learning. Table 3.2 shows the individual questions that comprise each subscale and the comprehensive megascale. The Good Teaching and Academic Challenge megascales are used in the first stage of my analysis to answer the first research question. The individual subscales are then used in the second stage of my analysis to answer the second research question.

Dependent Variables.   The dependent variables in this analysis represent two liberal arts outcomes investigated as part of the Wabash National Study: leadership and psychological well-being. Each of these relate to the students' personal development and their relationships with others.

Leadership was assessed with the 68-item, revised version two of the Socially Responsible Leadership Scale (SRLS), which measures the eight dimensions of Astin's Social Change Model of leadership development (Astin & Astin, 1996). According to this model, leadership is a collaborative group process that promotes positive social change in an organization or community (Tyree, 1998). Individuals who demonstrate strong socially responsible leadership capabilities are self-aware, act in accordance with personal values and beliefs, invest time and energy in activities that they believe are important, work with diverse others to accomplish common goals, have a sense of civic and social responsibility, and desire to make the world a better place. The instrument has eight scales corresponding to the eight dimensions of leadership specified in the Astin and Astin (1996) model: Consciousness of Self, Congruence, Commitment, Collaboration, Common Purpose, Controversy with Civility, Citizenship, and Change. An overall leadership scale combines all eight of the subscales. The SRLS was developed specifically to

Table 3.1. Good Teaching Comprehensive Megascale (alpha = 0.92)

Subscale: Faculty Interest in Students (alpha = 0.85)
Most faculty with whom R had contact are:
- genuinely interested in students
- interested in helping students grow in more than just academic areas
- outstanding teachers
- genuinely interested in teaching
- willing to spend time outside of class to discuss issues of interest and importance to students

Subscale: Prompt Academic Feedback (alpha = 0.68)
- How often faculty informed R of level of performance in a timely manner
- How often has R received prompt written or oral feedback from faculty on academic performance
- How often faculty checked to see if R had learned the material well before going on to new material

Subscale: Positive Nonclassroom Interactions with Faculty (alpha = 0.85)
The extent R agrees that nonclassroom interactions with faculty have had a positive influence on:
- personal growth, values, and attitudes
- intellectual growth and interest in ideas
- career goals and aspirations

The extent R agrees that he or she:
- has developed a close, personal relationship with at least one faculty member
- is satisfied with the opportunities to meet and interact informally with faculty members

Subscale: Teaching Clarity (alpha = 0.89)
Frequency that:
- faculty gave clear explanations
- faculty made good use of examples and illustrations to explain difficult points
- faculty effectively reviewed and summarized the material
- faculty interpreted abstract ideas and theories clearly
- faculty gave assignments that helped R learn the course material
- the presentation of material was well-organized
- faculty were well-prepared for class
- class time was used effectively
- course goals and requirements were clearly explained
- faculty had a good command of what they were teaching

measure leadership in college students. The internal consistency reliabilities for the eight subscales of the SRLS in the present study ranged from 0.77 to 0.88. Each of the subscales and the overall leadership scale are used as dependent variables in my models.

Psychological well-being was assessed using the Ryff Scales of Psychological Well-Being (SPWB; Ryff, 1989; Ryff & Keyes, 1995), a 54-item, theoretically grounded instrument that focuses on six dimensions of psychological well-being. Subscales of the SPWB measure: positive evaluations of oneself (Self-Acceptance), sense of continued growth and development as a person (Personal Growth), belief in a purposeful and meaningful life (Purpose in Life), quality relations with others (Positive Relations), capacity to effectively manage one's life and surrounding world

Table 3.2. Academic Challenge Comprehensive Megascale (alpha = 0.88)

Subscale: Student's Academic Effort (alpha = 0.65)
- In a typical week, the number of problem sets that takes R *more* than an hour to complete
- The extent to which examinations during the current school year challenged R to do his/her best work
- Number of hours per week R spends preparing for class
- Extent to which R's institution emphasizes spending significant amounts of time studying and on academic work

How often has R:
- worked harder than R thought he/she could to meet an instructor's standards or expectations
- asked questions or contributed to class discussions
- made a class presentation
- prepared two or more drafts of a paper or assignment before turning it in
- come to class without completing readings or assignments (reverse-coded)

During current year:
- the number of assigned textbooks, books, or book-length packs of course readings that R read
- the number of written papers or reports between five and 19 pages that R wrote

Subscale: Higher Order Thinking (alpha = 0.76)
How often have exams or assignments required R to:
- write essays
- use course content to address a problem not presented in the course
- compare or contrast topics or ideas from a course
- point out the strengths and weaknesses of a particular argument or point of view
- argue for or against a particular point of view and defend an argument

Subscale: Classes Challenge Thinking (alpha = 0.82)
- How often students challenged each other's ideas in class

How often faculty:
- asked challenging questions in class
- asked R to show how a particular course concept could be applied to an actual problem or situation
- asked R to point out any fallacies in basic ideas, principles, or points of view presented in the course
- asked R to argue for or against a point of view
- challenged R's ideas in class

Subscale: Integrative Learning (alpha = 0.76)
The extent R agrees that courses have helped R:
- understand the historical, political, and social connections of past events
- see the connections between intended career and how it affects society

The extent R agrees that out-of-class experiences have helped R:
- connect what was learned in the classroom with life events
- translate knowledge and understanding from the classroom into action

How often has R:
- worked on a paper or project that required integrating ideas or information from various sources
- put together ideas or concepts from different courses when completing assignments or during class discussions
- discussed ideas from readings or classes with others outside of class (students, family members, coworkers, etc.)

Time spent:
- synthesizing and organizing ideas, information, or experiences into new, more complex interpretations and relationships
- making judgments about the value of information, arguments, or methods, such as examining how others gathered and interpreted data and assessing the soundness of their conclusions

NEW DIRECTIONS FOR INSTITUTIONAL RESEARCH • DOI: 10.1002/ir

(Environmental Mastery), and sense of self-determination (Autonomy; Keyes, Shmotkin, & Ryff, 2002; Ryff, 1989; Ryff & Keyes, 1995). The six 9-item scales have internal consistency reliabilities ranging from 0.83 to 0.91 (C. Ryff, personal communication, August 2004). Each of the subscales and the overall psychological well-being scale are used as dependent variables in my models.

Analysis. In the first stage of the analysis, I regressed each leadership and psychological well-being outcome on the Good Teaching megascale and the Academic Challenge megascale, along with all of the independent variables, using two separate samples: White students ($N = 5,846$) and African-American students ($N = 764$). All regressions included the following variables: male, low family income, first-generation status, high school ACT score, academic motivation, number of liberal arts courses taken, regional college, research university, 2007 cohort, 2008 cohort, pretest for the outcome, Good Teaching scale, Academic Challenge scale, Positive Peer Interactions scale, and Diverse Experiences scale.

By using two separate samples, the findings illustrate patterns of experience for different groups of students (Stage, 2007), which provides practical data for campus administrators. The alternative, to simply include race in a general effects model, would demonstrate that there are differences on the outcome by race, but does not illustrate which experiences lead to those differences. After running the regressions, I tested to see whether the coefficients for Good Teaching and Academic Challenge were statistically significantly different between the two groups (Paternoster, Brame, Mazerolle, & Piquero, 1998). Because I found that the effects of Good Teaching and Academic Challenge differed between White and African-American students on several outcomes, I ran a second stage of analysis to try to understand more about those differences.

In the second stage, instead of using the Good Teaching and Academic megascales, I regressed each outcome on four Good Teaching subscales (Faculty Interest in Students, Prompt Academic Feedback, Positive Nonclassroom Interactions with Faculty, and Teaching Clarity) and four Academic Challenge subscales (Student's Academic Effort, Higher Order Thinking, Classes Challenge Thinking, and Integrative Learning), along with the rest of the independent variables listed above. Then I tested to see if the effects of the Good Teaching subscales and Academic Challenge subscales were significantly different for African-American and White students (Paternoster et al., 1998).

In all regression analyses I used listwise deletion due to the relatively small amount of missing data. I weighted the data based on sex, race, and ACT scores to represent the first-year class at each institution during the year the students entered, thereby making the sample more similar to the population it represents. Finally, I used the survey command in Stata software to designate institutions as the primary sampling units. Therefore, standard errors were calculated using degrees of freedom representing the number of institutions instead of the number of students, thereby reducing

**Table 3.3. The Effects of Good Teaching on Leadership and
Psychological Well-Being Outcomes for White and African-American
Students**

	White	African American	Sig Dif
Leadership Outcomes			
Change	0.07**	−0.04	N
Citizenship	0.09**	0.04	N
Collaboration	0.15**	0.08*	N
Commitment	**0.19****	**0.03**	**Y**
Common Purpose	0.17**	0.07	N
Congruence	**0.15****	**0.02**	**Y**
Consciousness of Self	0.09**	0.05	N
Controversy with Civility	**0.15****	**−0.02**	**Y**
Overall Leadership Score	**0.16****	**0.04**	**Y**
Psychological Well-Being Outcomes			
Autonomy	0.05**	0.07	N
Environmental Mastery	0.13**	0.08	N
Personal Growth	0.11**	−0.01	N
Positive Relations	**0.09****	**−0.03**	**Y**
Purpose in Life	0.15**	0.08	N
Self-Acceptance	0.14**	0.09*	N
Overall Well-Being Score	0.14**	0.05	N

Note: Y in the Sig Dif column indicates that the coefficients for White and African-American students are significantly different from each other.
*$p < .05$. **$p < .01$.

the chance of Type I error (finding significance where there is not any).
This type of adjustment is necessary because students within institutions
are more alike than students at different institutions (Groves et al., 2004).

Findings

Table 3.3 shows the b coefficients for the effect of Good Teaching on
leadership and psychological well-being outcomes for White and African-
American students during the first year of college. The "Sig Dif" column
indicates whether the coefficients for White and African-American students
significantly differ. The effects of Good Teaching on Commitment, Congruence, Controversy with Civility, Overall Leadership, and Positive Relations
are all positive for White students and not significant for African-American
students. There were no equations in which the effect of Good Teaching on
the outcomes was greater for African-American students than White students. Furthermore, while Good Teaching had a significant effect on all of
the outcomes for White students, it was significant on only two of the outcomes for African-American students—Collaboration and Self-Acceptance.
    Table 3.4 shows the b coefficients for the effect of Academic Chal-
lenge on leadership and psychological well-being outcomes for White and

Table 3.4. The Effects of Academic Challenge on Leadership and Psychological Well-Being Outcomes for White and African-American Students

	White	African American	Sig Dif
Leadership Outcomes			
Change	**0.10****	**0.33****	**Y**
Citizenship	0.15**	0.19**	N
Collaboration	**0.10****	**0.22****	**Y**
Commitment	**0.11****	**0.30****	**Y**
Common Purpose	**0.11****	**0.26****	**Y**
Congruence	**0.08****	**0.22****	**Y**
Consciousness of Self	**0.09****	**0.17****	**Y**
Controversy with Civility	**0.07****	**0.25****	**Y**
Overall Leadership Score	**0.13****	**0.29****	**Y**
Psychological Well-Being Outcomes			
Autonomy	0.06**	0.11**	N
Environmental Mastery	0.08**	0.13*	N
Personal Growth	0.10**	0.23**	N
Positive Relations	0.04*	0.13**	N
Purpose in Life	0.12**	0.14*	N
Self-Acceptance	**0.05***	**0.18****	**Y**
Overall Well-Being Score	0.09**	0.18**	N

Note: Y in the Sig Dif column indicates that the coefficients for White and African-American students are significantly different from each other.
*p < .05. **p < .01.

African-American students during the first year of college. Academic Challenge had a significant effect on all of the outcomes for both groups of students. The "Sig Dif" column indicates whether the coefficients for White and African-American students significantly differ. The effects of Academic Challenge were significantly greater for African-American students than White students on eight of the nine leadership outcomes and one of the psychological well-being outcomes. There were no equations in which the effect of Academic Challenge on the outcomes was greater for White students than African-American students.

Table 3.5 shows the *b* coefficients for the effects of four Good Teaching subscales (Faculty Interest in Students, Prompt Academic Feedback, Positive Nonclassroom Interactions with Faculty, and Teaching Clarity) on leadership and psychological well-being outcomes during the first year of college. All coefficients in the table represent statistically different effects for White and African-American students; findings that did not indicate a significant difference between groups are not presented. In general, the effects of Faculty Interest in Students tend to be significant and negative for African-American students and not significant for White students, with the exception of the effect on Commitment, which was positive for White students and not significant for African-American students. The effects of Teaching Clarity tend to be significant and positive for White students and

Table 3.5. Significant Differences Between White and African-American Students for the Effects of Four Good Teaching Subscales on Leadership and Psychological Well-Being Outcomes

	Faculty Interest in Students	
	White	African American
Leadership Outcomes		
Change	−0.01	−0.11**
Commitment	0.07*	−0.09
Congruence	0.04	−0.09*
Total Leadership	0.02	−0.08*
Psychological Well-Being Outcomes		
Positive Relations	0.03	−0.07**

	Prompt Academic Feedback	
	White	African American
Leadership Outcomes		
Congruence	−0.06*	0.11
Consciousness of Self	−0.02	0.10

	Positive Nonclassroom Interactions with Faculty	
No significantly different effects		

	Teaching Clarity	
	White	African American
Leadership Outcomes		
Commitment	0.18**	0.01
Common Purpose	0.17**	0.04
Congruence	0.16**	0.03
Psychological Well-Being Outcomes		
Autonomy	0.05**	0.11**
Personal Growth	0.10**	−0.04

Note: Findings that did not indicate a significant difference between groups are not presented in this table.
*$p < .05$. **$p < .01$.

not significant for African-American students, with the exception of the effect on Autonomy, which was positive for both groups. There were few significantly different effects of Prompt Academic Feedback and no significantly different effects of Positive Nonclassroom Interactions with Faculty.

Table 3.6 shows the b coefficients for the effects of four Academic Challenge subscales (Student's Academic Effort, Higher Order Thinking, Classes Challenge Thinking, and Integrative Learning) on leadership and psychological well-being outcomes during the first year of college. All coefficients in the table represent statistically significant different effects for White and African-American students; findings that did not indicate a significant

Table 3.6. Significant Differences Between White and African-American Students for the Effects of Four Academic Challenge Subscales on Leadership and Psychological Well-Being Outcomes

	Student's Academic Effort	
	White	African American
Leadership Outcomes		
Congruence	0.07*	−0.10
Controversy with Civility	−0.01	−0.13*
Psychological Well-Being Outcomes		
Purpose in Life	0.12**	0.00
Total Well-Being	0.08**	−0.01

	Higher Order Thinking
No significantly different effects	

	Classes Challenge Thinking	
	White	African American
Leadership Outcomes		
Change	0.01	0.22**
Collaboration	−0.02	0.18**
Commitment	−0.01	0.27**
Common Purpose	−0.02	0.24**
Congruence	−0.02	0.17**
Consciousness of Self	0.00	0.16**
Controversy with Civility	0.01	0.26**
Total Leadership	0.00	0.24**
Psychological Well-Being Outcomes		
Environmental Mastery	−0.02	0.12*
Personal Growth	0.00	0.15*
Positive Relations	−0.02	0.10*
Purpose in Life	−0.03*	0.12*
Self-Acceptance	−0.04	0.15**
Total Well-Being	−0.02	0.15**

	Integrative Learning	
	White	African American
Leadership Outcomes		
Change	0.07*	0.24**
Congruence	0.07*	0.19**

Note: Findings that did not indicate a significant difference between groups are not presented in this table.
$*p < .05. **p < .01.$

difference between groups are not presented. The effects of Student's Academic Effort are significant and positive for White students and not significant for African-American students with the exception of Controversy with Civility, which is negatively affected for African-American students and not significantly affected for White students. In general, Classes that Challenge Thinking are significant and positive for African-American students and not significant for White students, with the exception of Purpose in Life that is significant and negative. The effects of Integrative Thinking are significant and positive for both groups, but have a much greater effect for African-American students. There are no significant differences of the effect of Higher Order Thinking between White and African-American students.

Discussion

The first stage of my analysis replicated prior findings that suggest that the effects of Good Teaching and Academic Challenge on leadership and psychological well-being differ for White and African-American students during the first year of college (Goodman, 2010). Where differences occurred, Good Teaching tended to be more beneficial for White students than African-American students, whereas Academic Challenge tended to be more beneficial to African-American students than White students. Academic Challenge had a significant effect on all of the outcomes for both groups, while Good Teaching had a significant effect on all of the outcomes for White students, but only two outcomes for African-American students.

The second stage of my analysis further identified specific aspects of teaching and challenge that differ on the effects of the outcomes for the two groups. Teaching Clarity appeared to be the most important aspect of good teaching when it comes to leadership development and psychological well-being for students in their first year of college. Surprisingly, Faculty Interest in Students only positively affected one outcome for White students and negatively affected several outcomes for African-American students. These results bring into question whether the highly recommended practice of "good teaching" is of primary benefit mostly to White students.

When it comes to Academic Challenge, Classes that Challenge Thinking had a positive effect on all of the outcomes for African-American students, but not White students. Integrative Learning had a positive effect on two outcomes for both groups, though it had a larger effect for African-American students compared to White students. Within the Academic Challenge models, only Student's Academic Effort has a more positive effect for White students than African-American students on some of the outcomes. In general, these findings suggest that during the first year of college, good teaching primarily benefited White students, while academic challenge benefited African-American students on the personal and interpersonal growth associated with leadership and psychological well-being outcomes.

Good practices in undergraduate education have been widely lauded and subsequently incorporated into surveys that many campuses routinely administer to their first-year students (Chickering & Gamson, 1999; Kuh et al., 2005; Pascarella, 2008; Pascarella et al., 2004). This study suggests that in order to understand how those practices are benefiting students, institutional researchers should test for conditional effects or disaggregate data based on relevant student characteristics. This is especially true for institutions that have concerns about the academic success or retention of particular groups of students, such as first-generation, low-income, students of color, low academic preparation, etc. By using NSSE or Wabash National Study data to analyze the potentially differing effects of good practices on first-year outcomes for different groups of students, institutions can begin to understand which practices benefit whom and which practices are less effective.

This research is not the first to suggest the importance of looking for conditional effects or disaggregating data for analysis. A growing group of researchers focused on bringing critical perspectives to quantitative studies has suggested that differences by race should be accounted for in more higher education research (Stage, 2007). Pascarella (2006) has suggested that while research in the 1990s has started to look for conditional effects between groups, that type of analysis must become a routine aspect of inquiry in order to prevent differing experiences between groups from being masked. Mayhew and Briscoe (2009) demonstrated that even results of factor analysis can vary when conducted on samples of different racial groups. This research adds to existing evidence suggesting the importance of trying to understand how different groups of students experience college. This is especially true when studying first-year students, whom educators want to persist in their studies and build a good foundation for learning over the course of four years.

Institutions that use research to discern the differing effects of student experiences for different groups of students can take action to make sure all students gain the most they can from their first year of college. For example, the findings from this study could influence academic advising, faculty development, and first-year seminars. Advisors aware of different experiences of teaching and challenge could ask their advisees about their own experiences in those areas and help them make sense of their experiences in a way that would benefit them. Faculty development centers could react to the findings from this study by incorporating topics of teaching clarity and integrative learning into their programs. Finally, those who work in first-year seminars could explicitly discuss academic challenge with the students they work with, in order to find ways to help those who are not benefiting from challenge to understand it in a new way and learn to react to it positively.

Good practices in undergraduate education have followed a trajectory from when they were first articulated in the late 1980s. They have been voraciously promoted since that time, adapted for student affairs practice, and incorporated into measures within research that informs educators and practitioners. The next phase of understanding the relevance of good practices to student success requires routinely studying the differential effects of those practices for different student populations. By understanding those differential effects, educators and practitioners can adapt educational behaviors and environments to maximize the benefits for all students. This is especially important for first-year students, to help them create a strong foundation for their educational journey and persist to graduation. The role of institutional researchers is vital to understanding who benefits from which practices during the first year of college.

References

Astin, H. S., & Astin, A. W. (1996). *A social change model of leadership development: Guidebook* (Version III). Los Angeles: Higher Education Research Institute, University of California at Los Angeles.

Blimling, G. S., Whitt, E. J., & Associates. (1999). *Good practice in student affairs: Principles to foster student learning*. San Francisco, CA: Jossey-Bass.

Chickering, A. W., & Gamson, Z. F. (1987). Seven principles for good practice in undergraduate education. *AAHE Bulletin, 39*(7), 3–7.

Chickering, A. W., & Gamson, Z. F. (Eds.). (1991). *New Directions for Teaching and Learning: No. 47. Applying the seven principles for good practice in higher education*. San Francisco, CA: Jossey-Bass.

Chickering, A. W., & Gamson, Z. F. (1999). Development and adaptations of the seven principles for good practice in undergraduate education. In M. D. Svinicki (Ed.), *New Directions for Teaching and Learning: No. 80. Teaching and learning on the edge of the millennium: Building on what we have learned* (pp. 75–81). San Francisco, CA: Jossey-Bass.

Goodman, K. (2010). *The effects of good practices on liberal arts outcomes: An analysis of three cohorts of WNSLAE data*. Report prepared for project manager, Charles Blaich. Iowa City, IA: Center for Research on Undergraduate Education.

Groves, R. M., Fowler, F. J., Jr., Couper, M. P., Lepkowski, J. M., Singer, E., & Tourangeau, R. (2004). *Survey methodology*. Hoboken, NJ: Wiley.

Hurtado, S., Milem, J. F., Clayton-Pedersen, A. R., & Allen, W. R. (1998). Enhancing campus climates for racial/ethnic diversity: Educational policy and practice. *Review of Higher Education, 21*(3), 279–302.

Keyes, C., Shmotkin, D., & Ryff, C. (2002). Optimizing well-being: The empirical encounter of two traditions. *Journal of Personality and Social Psychology, 82*, 1007–1022.

Kuh, G. D., Kinzie, J., Schuh, J. H., Whitt, E. J., & Associates. (2005). *Student success in college: Creating conditions that matter*. San Francisco, CA: Jossey-Bass.

Mayhew, M. J., & Briscoe, K. (2009, November). *Rethinking campus climate: How we privilege White perceptions and experiences through the questions we ask and the analytic techniques we use*. Paper presented at the Annual Conference of the Association for the Study of Higher Education, Vancouver, BC.

Pascarella, E. T. (2006). How college affects students: Ten directions for future research. *Journal of College Student Development, 47*(5), 508–520.

Pascarella, E. T. (2008). *Methodological report for Wabash National Study of Liberal Arts Education*. Retrieved from http://www.liberalarts.wabash.edu/storage/WNSLAE _Research_Methods_March_2008.pdf

Pascarella, E. T., Wolniak, G. C., Cruce, T. M., & Blaich, C. F. (2004). Do liberal arts colleges really foster good practices in undergraduate education? *Journal of College Student Development, 45*(1), 57–74.

Paternoster, R., Brame, R., Mazerolle, P., & Piquero, A. (1998). Using the correct statistical test for the equality of regression coefficients. *Criminology, 36*(4), 859–866.

Ryff, C. (1989). Happiness is everything, or is it? Explorations on the meaning of psychological well-being. *Journal of Personality and Social Psychology, 57*, 1069–1081.

Ryff, C., & Keyes, C. (1995). The structure of psychological well-being revisited. *Journal of Personality and Social Psychology, 69*, 719–727.

Seifert, T. A., Goodman, K. M., King, P. M., & Baxter Magolda, M. B. (2010). Using mixed methods to study first-year college impact on liberal arts learning outcomes. *Journal of Mixed Methods Research, 4*(3), 248–267.

Stage, F. K. (2007). Answering critical questions using quantitative data. In F. K. Stage (Ed.), *New Directions for Institutional Research: No. 133. Using quantitative data to answer critical questions* (pp. 5–16). San Francisco, CA: Jossey-Bass.

Tyree, T. (1998). *Designing an instrument to measure socially responsible leadership using the social change model of leadership development* (Unpublished doctoral dissertation). University of Maryland, College Park.

KATHLEEN M. GOODMAN *is an assistant professor of student affairs in higher education at Miami University.*

NEW DIRECTIONS FOR INSTITUTIONAL RESEARCH • DOI: 10.1002/ir

4

In this chapter findings from a nationally representative longitudinal study offer insights into how the experiences students have during their first college year affect their intention to be retained at their initial college for the second year.

Programs and Practices That Retain Students From the First to Second Year: Results From a National Study

Linda DeAngelo

Introduction

Reforming and improving the first-year college experience has been a focus of retention efforts on college campuses since the 1980s. Much of this reform has been at the program level (Alexander & Gardner, 2009), and on many, if not most, college campuses new first-year curricula, layered with more traditional general education and introductory courses for the major, are now the normative classroom experience during the first college year. Among the curricula that have now become standard fare during the first year are learning communities, first-year seminars, and service learning. Though the potential of these types of curricula has been well documented (see Upcraft, Gardner, Barefoot, & Associates, 2005), and studies indicate that these innovations are efficacious (see Kuh, 2008; Pascarella & Terenzini, 2005), some recent studies find that these curricula have little direct impact on student learning and development (see DeAngelo & Hurtado, 2009; Pike, Hansen, & Lin, 2011; Rocconi, 2011). Thus, there is still much to learn about how participating in these experiences affects students. Indeed, as noted by Alexander and Gardner (2009), because many of these efforts still operate at the margins of campus, they may not have much of an effect on students.

Given the effort that campuses have put into reforming their first-year curricula so as to maximize retention, there is a tremendous need for further studies examining how these curricular changes affect retention. This study is intended to begin to fill in this research gap. Understanding first-year retention is also important since, as noted by Tinto (1993), college attrition is most likely to occur during or immediately following the first year of

New Directions for Institutional Research, no. 160 © 2014 Wiley Periodicals, Inc.
Published online in Wiley Online Library (wileyonlinelibrary.com) • DOI: 10.1002/ir.20061

college. As reported by ACT (2011), at four-year colleges the probability that a first-year student will not return for their second year is approximately 25%.

Research Background

While studies examining the first-year experience and specifically first-year curricula and involvements are very much needed, the research literature on retention is well developed. Most studies of persistence rely on Tinto's (1975, 1987, 1993) theory of student departure. Tinto proposes a longitudinal model of persistence that takes into account precollege student characteristics and involvement and engagement in the college environment, examining how academic and social integration into the campus community affects retention. Through his research, Tinto (1996) identified seven factors that explain why students decide not to return to campus: (a) academic difficulties; (b) adjustment difficulties; (c) uncertain, narrow, or new goals; (d) external commitments; (e) financial concerns; (f) lack of student–institution fit; and (g) isolation from campus life. In regard to these areas, researchers have generally found that they are predictors of retention. In addition, research has generally found that the effects of student background characteristics on retention are mostly indirect and that once the college experience is controlled, these factors are less important.

While much is known about retention generally, much less is known about how participation in first-year curricula affects the retention decision. Tinto's (1997) more recent research connects learning community participation and retention. Generally, as reviewed by Pascarella and Terenzini (2005), studies of learning communities and living learning communities show that they positively affect retention, though literature studying the relationship of participation and first-year persistence is sparse and mixed. Kanoy and Bruhn's (1996) and Pike, Schroder, and Berry's (1997) studies examined living learning communities and first-year retention specifically, and both found that participation did not have a direct effect on retention. Though this was the case, the Pike et al. study did find that participation has an indirect effect on retention through its effect on academic integration, and the Kanoy and Bruhn study found that participation was positively linked to higher grades in the first two years of college.

First-year seminars have received more treatment in the literature than learning communities, and the large majority of these studies show a strong positive link between participation and first-year retention. However, as discussed by Pascarella and Terenzini (2005), many of these studies lack sufficient controls for student background characteristics and self-selection bias. Still, even in studies with matched samples (Boudreau & Kromrey, 1994; Schnell & Doetkott, 2003) and experiential design (Strumph & Hunt, 1993) the findings support the positive link between first-year seminar participation and retention. In one of the only multi-institution studies with sufficient controls, Gilmartin and Sax (2002) found no effect on retention to the sophomore year for participation in a first-year seminar. In a single institution study with fewer controls, Handel (2001) found similar results.

Though the positive benefits of service learning are well established and show consistent positive connection between participation and learning and cognitive growth (Astin, Vogelgesang, Ikeda, & Yee, 2000), the relationship of service learning to first-year retention has yet to be examined. Regarding participation in service learning, Kuh (2008) found that students who participated in service learning during their first year had higher learning gains on average than students who did not have this experience. He found similar results for participation in learning communities and first-year seminars and named these three experiences as high-impact practices for first-year students.

Research Objective

Using past research as a guide, this study is intended to expand our understanding of how the first-year experience inside and outside of the classroom affects student retention, specifically the intent to return to one's initial college for the second year. Although intent to reenroll is not a direct measure of retention, Bean's (1980, 1982, 1983) research indicates that intention to return is a very powerful predictor of actual retention. Focusing on the programs and practices that have been central to the first-year curriculum reforms of the last three decades, the research question guiding this study is:

- Controlling for student background characteristics/experiences and the institution attended, what effect do first-year experiences inside and outside of the classroom have on intent to persist at the same college for the second year?

Methodology

This section details the data and research design for this study.

Data Source and Sample.   Data were derived from the Cooperative Institutional Research Program's (CIRP) 2007 Freshman Survey (TFS) and 2008 Your First College Year (YFCY) survey. CIRP is housed at the Higher Education Research Institute (HERI) at the University of California, Los Angeles and has been collecting data on college students for more than 40 years. The TFS is administered during summer orientation or the first few weeks of class, and the YFCY is administered to students at the end of the first year of college. In total, over 26,000 students from 487 four-year institutions participated in both surveys, constituting a longitudinal data set of the first year of college.

For the first time in its history, CIRP weighted the longitudinal YFCY data set to represent the national population of students at four-year institutions who complete the first year of college. Data from Integrated Postsecondary Education Data System (IPEDS) on fall-to-fall first-time full-time retention rates for first-year students were used to represent the national population. Thus, the sample of students for weighting was limited to first-time, full-time students in both fall 2007 and spring 2008, slightly reducing the sample to 25,602 students. The weighting technique employed adjusts the sample upward to the population (Babbie, 2001; Dey, 1997), taking into account individual as well as institutional response bias. For a detailed description of the weighting procedures and variables used in the weighting, please contact the Higher Education Research Institute at www.heri.ucla.edu.

Missing Data.   In order to preserve the full national longitudinal data set in its near entirety, an expectation-maximization (EM) algorithm was used to compensate for missing values. This method provides a more accurate estimation for missing data than options such as replacing missing values with the mean value for the variable across respondents (McLachlan & Krishnan, 1997). Data for gender, other dichotomous independent variables, and the dependent variable were not imputed and cases with missing data on these variables were deleted. This created a final nationally representative longitudinal data set of 24,443 students for this study.

Study Variables.   A full list of the variables used in this study is provided in Appendix 4.1. The outcome variable, taken from the YFCY, asks: "What do you think you will be doing in fall 2008?" Possible responses were: "attending your current (or most recent) institution," "attending another institution," "don't know/have not yet decided," and "not attending any institution." For the purposes of this study, students who answered "attending your current (or most recent) institution" were coded as 1 and students who answered "attending another institution" or "not attending any institution" were coded as 0. Students who were undecided about their decision were not included in the analysis.

Key independent variables were intended to capture the effect of recent undergraduate curriculum reform efforts on the intent students have to reenroll for the second year of college. Many of these curriculum reform efforts were intended to enhance the first-year experience and aid in within-institution retention. This study includes variables to measure the effect of first-year housing, participation in service learning, learning communities, and first-year seminars designed to assist students in adjusting to college.

This study also includes a set of key variables intended to capture student experiences and behaviors outside of the classroom, all of which have been linked to learning outcomes of a liberal education (AACU, 2007). These variables include discussing course content with students outside of class, studying with other students, working on a professor's research project, having meaningful and honest discussions about race/ethnic relations outside of class with students from racial/ethnic groups other than your own, and having intellectual discussions outside of class with students from racial/ethnic groups other than your own.

Other first-year experience variables include three measures of classroom behaviors as captured by the latent variable CIRP Constructs: ease of academic adjustment, habits of mind, and academic disengagement. The CIRP Constructs were created and scored using Item Response Theory (IRT; see Sharkness, DeAngelo, & Pryor [2010] for details on the methods used to create the CIRP Constructs). In addition, this study includes a CIRP Construct measuring student–faculty interaction and variables measuring the effect of college grade point average (GPA), working full-time, and financial concerns at the end of the first year of college.

Data Analyses.   This study used blocked binary logistic regression in STATA 11 to predict intent to reenroll for the second year of college at the same institution. This statistical approach permits the researcher to analyze more effectively how a particular set of experiences influences an educational choice, while simultaneously controlling for confounding factors (Cabrera, 1994), and it is the appropriate method when a dependent variable is dichotomous (Hosmer & Lemeshow, 2000). In this study, the variables were blocked into five groups: (a) control variables, (b) residence and employment status, (c) classroom experiences/behaviors, (d) experiences/behavior outside of the classroom, and (e) academic achievement and financial concerns at the end of the first year of college. This method of logistic regression was chosen in order to allow for a more nuanced understanding of how the experiences students have during the first year of college affect their intent to reenroll for the second year of college. Based on the results of the blocked logistic regression, an additional logistic regression with interaction terms related to the effect of discussing course content with other students outside of class and gender, housing, and first-year seminars was completed. For the variables that were found to be significant, delta-p statistics (Peterson, 1985) were used to calculate the predicted probability of returning after the first year for each variable while holding all of the other variables constant at their observed values. For continuous and quasicontinuous variables, the delta-p signifies the incremental change in probability in the dependent variable for a one-unit increase in the independent variable; whereas for binary variables, the delta-p calculates the predicted probability of the dependent variable occurring, in this case intent to return to college for the second year.

Results and Discussion

The overall probability that a student who completes the first year of college intends to return to their initial institution for the second year is 94%. Though high, this nationally weighted figure is in a range that is consistent with what would be expected based on other studies (Gilmartin & Sax, 2002; Herzog, 2005; Nora, Cabrera, Hagedorn, & Pascarella, 1996).

As the probability that students who begin college at four-year institutions will not return for their sophomore year is 25% (ACT, 2011), this suggests that much of the first-year attrition risk occurs prior to the end of the first year. Though this study examines retention just among students who are successful in completing their first year, better understanding retention as it relates to this group is an important part of improving first to second year retention overall.

Results of the final logistic regression model with interaction terms are included in Table 4.1, and a summary of the coefficients at each regression step and in the final model is provided in Appendix 4.2. The final model shows the various control and study variables that significantly predict intent to reenroll at the same institution for the second year after the interaction terms are included in the model. Of the control variables only the likelihood of needing extra time to complete a degree, likelihood of transferring, attending a private institution, and institutional selectivity were significant. Of these, the likelihood of transfer and attending a private institution were negatively associated with the outcome, whereas the likelihood of needing extra time to complete a degree and institutional selectivity were positively associated with the outcome. The predicted probabilities or delta-p statistics, as displayed in Table 4.2, will aid in the interpretation of the regression. For a binary independent variable such as attending a private institution, the interpretation would be that the probability that a student attending a private institution intends to return after their first year is two percentage points lower than for a student at a public institution. For a quasicontinuous variable such as expectation of transferring, the interpretation would be that for each unit increase in the expectation of transferring the probability that a student intends to return to campus after their first year decreases by three percentage points.

First-Year Curriculum.   Based on results from the regression, it does not appear as if participation in service learning, learning communities, or first-year seminars has a direct effect on intent to return to one's initial college for the sophomore year. Rather than being an indictment of these new curricular efforts overall, perhaps as Alexander and Gardner (2009) suggest, these results have more to do with the uneven quality and placement of these programs at the margins of the campus curriculum. As Porter and Swing (2006) found in their study of the effect of first-year seminars on persistence, seminar quality does matter and is related to the persistence decision. In addition, since the intent of this curriculum is in part to assist students in gaining the types of skills necessary for success in college and to engage in the college experience meaningfully, perhaps the effects of these curricula are indirect or conditional in nature. As noted in Pascarella and Terenzini (2005), the potential conditional nature of these experiences has yet to be formally studied. Through the investigation of an interaction effect related to first-year seminars that is discussed in the next section, this research gap begins to be addressed.

NEW DIRECTIONS FOR INSTITUTIONAL RESEARCH • DOI: 10.1002/ir

Table 4.1. Final Logistic Model Predicting Intent to Persist to Sophomore Year

	Coefficient	SE	95% Confidence Interval	
Control variables				
Background				
Gender: female	0.266	0.325	−0.372	0.904
First generation: yes	−0.223	0.128	−0.473	0.028
Parental income	−0.036	0.020	−0.075	0.002
SAT comprehensive score	0.001	0.000	0.000	0.001
Retention risk entering freshman				
Financial concern				
(Reference group: none)				
Some	0.052	0.123	−0.189	0.294
Major	−0.040	0.216	−0.464	0.383
Likely need extra time to degree	0.169*	0.074	0.023	0.315
Likely transfer to different institution	−0.646***	0.058	−0.760	−0.532
Institution attended				
Institutional type: private	−0.291**	0.088	−0.463	−0.119
Institutional selectivity	0.002***	0.000	0.001	0.003
Study variables				
Residence and employment				
First-year housing				
(Reference group: first-year/special interest)				
Regular student housing	0.999**	0.358	0.296	1.700
Off-campus housing	1.326*	0.532	0.283	2.370
Worked full-time first year	−0.340*	0.168	−0.670	−0.010
First-year classroom engagement				
Ease of academic adjustment	−0.014*	0.007	−0.027	−0.001
Habits of mind for student success	−0.012	0.007	−0.027	0.002
Academic disengagement	−0.012	0.006	−0.025	0.000
Service learning				
(Reference group: not at all)				
Occasionally	0.087	0.107	−0.122	0.296
Frequently	0.355	0.219	−0.073	0.784
Learning community: yes	−0.116	0.123	−0.358	0.126
First-year seminar student success: yes	−0.819*	0.334	−1.474	−0.164
Engagement outside of the classroom				
Discuss course content with students				
(Reference group: not at all)				
Occasionally	1.341**	0.456	0.448	2.235
Frequently	1.571**	0.473	0.643	2.498
Studied with other students				
(Reference group: not at all)				
Occasionally	0.184	0.154	−0.117	0.486
Frequently	0.420*	0.174	0.079	0.760

(Continued)

NEW DIRECTIONS FOR INSTITUTIONAL RESEARCH • DOI: 10.1002/ir

Table 4.1. Continued

	Coefficient	SE	95% Confidence Interval	
Worked on professor's research project (Reference group: not at all)				
Occasionally	−0.287**	0.110	−0.503	−0.071
Frequently	0.053	0.211	−0.360	0.466
Had with other racial/ethnic groups				
Meaningful discussions about race	0.093	0.050	−0.004	0.191
Meaningful intellectual discussions	0.111*	0.050	0.014	0.208
Student–faculty interaction	0.028***	0.007	0.015	0.042
First-year academic achievement				
College GPA	0.160**	0.052	0.059	0.262
Retention risk at the end of first year				
Financial concern				
(Reference group: none)				
Some	0.098	0.125	−0.148	0.343
Major	−0.489**	0.171	−0.823	−0.155
Interaction terms				
Gender and discussing course content with students outside of class (Reference group: male and not at all)				
Female and occasionally	−0.644	0.346	−1.323	0.034
Female and frequently	−0.442	0.372	−1.171	0.287
Housing and discussing course content with students outside of class (Reference group: first year/special interest and not at all)				
Regular and occasionally	−1.048**	0.383	−1.799	−0.297
Regular and frequently	−1.175**	0.394	−1.947	−0.403
Off-campus and occasionally	−0.347	0.568	−1.461	0.767
Off-campus and frequently	−1.26*	0.616	−2.464	−0.051
First-year seminar and discussing course content with students outside of class (Reference group: no and not at all)				
Yes and occasionally	0.873*	0.352	0.183	1.564
Yes and frequently	0.860*	0.373	0.128	1.592
AIC	410174.100			
BIC	410506.300			
Degrees of freedom	41			

$N = 24{,}443$. Data have been weighted to represent the national sample of first-time, full-time freshmen who retained through year one.
*$p < .05$. **$p < .01$. ***$p < .001$.

Discussing Course Content With Other Students Outside of Class.

As the blocked logistic regression modeling progressed, discussing course content with other students outside of class occasionally or frequently as compared to not at all emerged as the most important first-year experience for understanding which students intend to return to their initial college

Table 4.2. Predicted Probabilities (Delta-*p* Values) of Significant Variables in the Final Model

Variable	Probability	Variable	Probability
Need extra time to degree	0.01	Work on professor's research project	
Transfer to different institution	−0.03	(Reference group: not at all)	0.95
Institutional type		Occasionally	0.93
(Reference group: public)	0.95	Frequently	0.95
Private	0.93	With other racial/ethnic groups	
Selectivity	<0.01	Intellectual discussions	0.01
Work full-time first year		College GPA	0.01
(Reference group: no)	0.94	Financial concern	
Yes	0.93	(Reference group: none)	0.95
		Some	0.95
Ease of academic adjust	<0.01	Major	0.92
Studied with other students			
(Reference group: not at all)	0.93		
Occasionally	0.94		
Frequently	0.95		

for the second year. In the fifth model (see Appendix 4.2), and prior to testing possible interaction effects with this variable, the probability that a student would return to campus for the sophomore year increased by four percentage points if they discussed course content occasionally, and by five percentage points if they engaged academically in this way frequently, as compared to not at all (results not shown). As the strongest predictor of intent to return to campus after the first year in the blocked logistic regression, this means that encouraging this type of academic engagement and facilitating this type of interaction is the single most important activity that colleges should consider in retention efforts aimed at the first year.

Although this type of engagement is positive and important to retention for all students, interaction term modeling shows that the benefit of this activity is also conditionally related to gender, place of residence, and participation in a first-year seminar. The conditional nature of this type of engagement to retention emerges in the fourth model (see Appendix 4.2) when this variable entered the regression. When this variable is entered, two suppressor effects are evident in the modeling. Women become significantly less likely than men to expect to return to their home campus for the second year, and the negative effect of living on campus in first-year/special interest housing as compared to off campus gets larger rather than smaller as expected with a normal effect.

Gender and Discussing Course Content With Other Students Outside of Class. Understanding how experiences on campus affect men and women differently is one of the important keys to improving degree

Table 4.3. Predicted Probability of the Effect of Gender, Housing, and First-Year Seminar by Discussing Course Content Outside of Class

	Gender		Housing			First-Year Seminar	
	Male	Female	First-Year	Regular	Off-Campus	No	Yes
Discussing course content							
Not at all	0.86	0.89	0.79	0.90	0.92	0.92	0.85
Occasionally	0.95	0.93	0.94	0.93	0.97	0.94	0.94
Frequently	0.95	0.94	0.95	0.95	0.96	0.95	0.95

completion rates, especially for men (Nora, Barlow, & Crisp, 2005). Currently women enjoy a 25% advantage over men in baccalaureate degree completion (DeAngelo, Franke, Hurtado, Pryor, & Tran, 2011), so keeping male students enrolled is a priority on most campuses. Uncovering that men are significantly more likely to intend to return to campus for the second year in the blocked logistic regression (see Appendix 4.2, model four) indicates the potential of an interaction effect. Results from the final model with the interaction term show that the interaction between gender and discussing course content outside of class does not reach statistical significance; neither of the individual interaction terms nor a post hoc test of the overall interaction term were significant. Despite this, and because of the importance of understanding a potential gender effect, an additional post hoc test of the interaction was completed. This test examines differences in the predicted probabilities of intent to return for women and men at the various levels of the discussing course content variable holding all other variables in the model constant at their observed values. Results from this procedure seem to indicate that men benefit from discussing course content outside of class more than women.

As shown in Table 4.3, at the "not at all" level the probability that a male student will return to campus is lower than for a female student, though the difference is not statistically significant. But, among those who discuss course content occasionally men are significantly more likely ($p = .001$) to intend to return to campus for the sophomore year than female students, and just as likely as female students to intend to return if they discuss course content frequently. All of this suggests that in terms of retention, male students stand to benefit more than female students from getting together outside of class with their peers to talk about the content of their courses. This discovery is particularly enlightening since data from this study show that among those who report not discussing course content outside of class, a much higher proportion are men (54%) than women (46%). Thus, encouraging this type of academic engagement among male students in particular may be one way to keep them on campus.

Housing and Discussing Course Content With Other Students Outside of Class. A boom in on-campus housing of first-year students and the development of residence halls and themed housing specifically devoted to first-year students is one of the outgrowths of the undergraduate reform efforts directed at improving the first college year. As noted in Zeller (2005), housing that is focused on the needs of first-year students is designed specifically to support student success by helping students connect in- and out-of-the classroom experiences. Past research on the first year indicates that there is a connection between living on campus and retention (Christie & Dinham, 1991; Wolfe, 1993), with degree attainment studies showing a connection between planning to live in a residence hall during first year and completing a degree (DeAngelo et al., 2011). In this study, results indicate that in terms of retention to the second year, it is not so much where a student lives during the first year but the fact that students who live on campus are more likely to be engaged in outside of the classroom activities such as discussing course content that has a relationship with retention. In looking at the data used in this study, only 37% of students who live off campus report discussing course content frequently compared to 42% of students in regular on-campus housing and 48% of students in first-year/special interest housing.

Repeating the process for the interaction with gender, an interaction term between the various types of housing and the various levels of discussing course content was added to the final logistic regression model. Three of the four interaction terms are significant and a post hoc test of the overall interaction term was also significant ($p = .006$). To investigate the effect further, predicted probabilities were calculated and post hoc test for significant differences in the probabilities was conducted, again holding all of the other variables constant at their observed values. As shown in Table 4.3, students who live in first-year/special interest housing who do not report discussing course content outside of class have the lowest probability of planning to return to campus for the second year, at just 79%. Results from the interaction and post hoc testing show that this probability is significantly lower than all of the other housing/discussing course content probabilities ($p < .05$ for all combinations). This means that students who are living in the housing situation designed to encourage engagement and who choose not to engage and get together to discuss the content of their courses with other students are at a particular risk for not returning to campus after their first year.

Additionally, for those students who live off campus but still find a way to meet with other students outside of class to discuss course content at least occasionally, the benefits of this engagement appear to be stronger in terms of retention than they do for students who live on campus and have the same level of engagement. The probability that a student who lives off campus and discusses course content occasionally will return to campus after the first year is significantly higher than the probability is for students

New Directions for Institutional Research • DOI: 10.1002/ir

who live on campus in first-year/special interest or in regular housing ($p <$ .001). Meaning that although off-campus students are less likely to discuss course content with other students outside of class, when they do have these engagements they actually stand to benefit more than students who live on campus. There is no statistical difference in the probabilities of returning to campus for the second year for the various types of housing for those who discuss course content frequently. For students who live off-campus, this type of academic engagement seems to be an important tie to the campus community that helps to keep them enrolled.

First-Year Seminars and Discussing Course Content With Other Students Outside of Class. Although there was no evidence of a potential interaction effect between first-year seminars and discussing course content outside of class in the blocked logistic regression, because first-year seminars are designed specifically to encourage the types of engagements that are connected to students' success (Hunter & Linder, 2005; Porter & Swing, 2006), an interaction term for first-year seminars and discussing course content was added to the final logistic regression model.[1] Both of the interaction terms are significant and the post hoc test of the overall interaction was significant ($p = .04$). The interaction terms show that students who take first-year seminars and discuss course content outside of class either frequently or occasionally are significantly more likely to intend to return for their second year than students who do not take a first-year seminar or discuss course content.

To investigate the effect further, predicted probabilities were calculated and a post hoc test for significant differences in the predicted probabilities was completed. Consistent with the earlier post hoc tests all of the other variables were held constant at their observed values. As shown in Table 4.3, the most interesting aspect of this interaction is that students who enroll in a first-year seminar and do not report discussing course content outside of class have a statistically significant ($p = .02$) and much lower probability of intending to return to campus than do students who likewise do not discuss course content but who do not take a first-year seminar, a probability difference of seven percentage points. Similar to the finding for housing, this indicates that students are at a particular risk of attrition when they are in an environment, in the first year, that is specifically designed to encourage their engagement and they choose not to engage. Although among students who reported that they did not discuss course content outside of class only a minority (41%) reported taking a first-year seminar, this finding is no less important. What all of this means is that first-year seminars are positively related to retention to the extent that they encourage students who would not otherwise discuss course content outside of class to engage in this activity. In addition, there is no statistical difference at either the occasional or frequent level of discussing course content between those who take and do not take a first-year seminar. Because of the presence of this interaction and the importance of understanding the effect of first-year curriculum on students, additional interactions with discussing course content and service learning and learning communities were attempted, but neither showed any signs of significance.

Other First-Year Experiences.   In addition to discussing course content with other students outside of class, three additional academic engagement experiences outside of the classroom were significantly related to intent to continue at the same institution for the second year. Compared to students who did not study with other students, students who reported this activity frequently were more likely to be retained, with a two percentage point boost in the probability of returning (see Table 4.2). Additionally, the more students interacted with faculty outside of class and the more they got together with students of other races/ethnicities for intellectual discussions, the more likely they were to intend to return following the first year. Interestingly, students who reported that they participated in research occasionally with faculty, rather than not at all, were significantly less likely to intend to return to campus after their first year, but there was no significant difference in retention expectations between those who engaged in this experience frequently and those who did not have this experience. The effect of academic achievement as measured by first-year grades was also significant, with a one percentage point increase in the probability of being retained for each incremental increase in GPA. This means that a C (1.75–2.24) student has a four percentage point lower probability of returning to campus as compared to an A (3.75–4.0) student.

With regard to financial concerns at the end of the first year, there is no significant difference between students who have some concerns and those who have no concerns, but students with major concerns (they don't think they will have enough funds) are significantly less likely than those with no financial concerns to expect to return to college for the second year. With a decreased probability of return of three percentage points, this means that despite all of the positive experiences students might have on campus that would propel them to continue, if students end their first year with significant concerns about their ability to finance their education they are at a serious attrition risk. This likely means that some institutions need to think more strategically about how they package financial aid in order not only to attract students to campus, but also to ensure they have enough funds to continue beyond the first year. This conclusion is supported by Herzog (2005) who found that students with unmet financial need at the end of the first year, particularly middle-income students, were at a higher attrition risk.

Conclusion and Implications

Three broad conclusions that can be drawn from this study will be of particular use to institutions as they continue to look for ways to improve retention and degree completion. First, although the potential of curriculum designed to enhance the first-year experience is vast, results from this study show that just having these curricular programs available for students is not enough. Institutions need to think more thoughtfully not only about the quality of their offerings but perhaps even more importantly about how well these experiences are integrated and central to the fabric of the institution. At its best and most successful, first-year curricula are part of a comprehensive campus-wide first-year initiative that has strong executive and administrative leadership and support from the entire campus community (Alexander & Gardner, 2009; Upcraft, Gardner, & Barefoot, 2005).

As discussed with regard to first-year seminars and discussing course content outside of class, it appears that for some students participation in these courses is encouraging them to engage academically outside of the classroom in a manner in which they might not have otherwise. Since the primary goal of this curriculum is creating conditions that are conducive to engaging in the types of academic experiences that will lead to success, certainly to this extent these courses, and specifically first-year seminars, are successful in producing retention. Future research will need to continue to examine the conditional and indirect effects of participating in service learning, learning communities, and first-year seminars, and will be improved if measures of quality as they relate to these experiences are included.

Second, the importance of engaging in meaningful academic engagement outside of the classroom is clearly the most important finding in this study. Students who get together with other students to talk about the content of their courses, who study together in groups, who interact intellectually with students from different races/ethnicities, and who interact with faculty are more likely to intend to persist and continue into the second year. In particular, the more students are getting together outside of the classroom to discuss the content of their courses, the higher the probability that they will persist to the second year. Although this type of interaction is salient and important for all students, findings from this study have vastly improved our understanding of who stands to benefit the most in terms of retention from this academic experience. Based on interaction term modeling and post hoc tests of the interactions, this outside-of-the-classroom experience benefits male students and students who live off campus the most. Since these two groups are at a higher attrition risk and less likely to earn a degree than their female and on-campus counterparts (DeAngelo et al., 2011), efforts by faculty and student affairs professionals to encourage this type of interaction and to create conditions that are conducive to this type of engagement will likely result in improved outcomes for these groups.

Third, campus professionals who interact with students, and in particular faculty and residence life staff, need to pay particular attention to students who seem to refrain from engaging academically outside of the classroom with their peers. Results from this study indicate that these students are at a very real attrition risk. Interaction term modeling and post hoc testing of the interactions show that students who participate in first-year seminars and who live in first-year/special interest housing and who choose for whatever reason not to engage outside of the classroom academically in conversations about their courses have a dramatically lower probability of returning to campus than do all other students. This lack of engagement even in the face of being in an environment designed to encourage it is a clear signal that intervention of some sort is needed.

As campuses continue look for ways to better serve their first-year students and increase success among this group, findings from this study can serve as a guide. A comprehensive approach to improving the first college year requires the strong involvement of everyone involved in both academic and student affairs (Alexander & Gardner, 2009; Upcraft, Gardner, & Barefoot, 2005), and attention to integrating experiences inside and outside of the classroom. The more that faculty and student affairs professionals can encourage students to engage academically with one another outside of the classroom, and the more they create environments that are conducive to this type of interaction, the greater the likelihood that students will persist to their second year.

Note

1. Model fit was significantly improved with this interaction in the model. In a model with just the gender and housing interactions, the fit statistics for BIC and AIC were 411230.7 and 410914.6, respectively; the DF was 39.

References

ACT. (2011). *Trends and tracking charts 1983–2010*. Retrieved from http://www.act.org/research/policymakers/pdf/10retain_trends.pdf

Alexander, J. S., & Gardner, J. N. (2009, May/June). Beyond retention: A comprehensive approach to the first college year. *About Campus, 14*(2), 18–26.

Association of American Colleges and Universities (AACU). (2007). *College level learning for the new global century: A report from the National Leadership Council for Liberal Education and America's Promise*. Washington, DC: Author.

Astin, A., Vogelgesang, L., Ikeda, E., & Yee, J. (2000). *How service learning affects students*. Los Angeles, CA: Higher Education Research Institute, UCLA.

Babbie, E. (2001). *The practice of social research*. Belmont, CA: Wadsworth.

Bean, J. P. (1980). Dropouts and turnover: The synthesis and test of a causal model of student attrition. *Research in Higher Education, 12*, 155–187.

Bean, J. P. (1982). Student attrition, intentions, and confidence: Interaction effects in a path model. *Research in Higher Education, 17*, 291–320.

Bean, J. P. (1983). The application of a model of turnover in work organizations to the student attrition process. *The Review of Higher Education, 6*, 129–148.

Boudreau, C., & Kromrey, J. (1994). A longitudinal study of the retention and academic performance of participants in a freshman orientation course. *Journal of College Student Development, 35*, 444–449.

Cabrera, A. F. (1994). Logistic regression analysis in higher education: An applied perspective. In J. C. Smart (Ed.), *Higher education: Handbook of theory and research* (Vol. 10, pp. 3225–3256). New York, NY: Agathon.

Christie, N. G., & Dinham, S. M. (1991). Institutional and external influences on social integration in the freshman year. *Journal of Higher Education, 62,* 412–436.

DeAngelo, L., Franke, R., Hurtado, S., Pryor, J. H., & Tran, S. (2011). *Completing college: Assessing graduation rates at four-year institutions.* Los Angeles, CA: Higher Education Research Institute, UCLA.

DeAngelo, L., & Hurtado, S. (2009, June). *Fostering "habits of mind" for student learning in the first-year of college: Results from a national study.* Paper presented at the Annual Meeting of the Association for Institutional Research, Atlanta, GA.

Dey, E. L. (1997). Working with low survey response rates: The efficacy of weighting adjustments. *Research in Higher Education, 38,* 215–227.

Gilmartin, S. K., & Sax, L. J. (2002, June). *What leads to dropping out after the first college year? Findings from the 2001 CIRP-YFCY national study of retention.* Paper presented at the annual meeting of the Association for Institutional Research, Toronto, Canada.

Handel, D. D. (2001, April). *The relative contribution of participating in a first-year seminar on student satisfaction and retention into the sophomore year.* Paper presented at the annual meeting of the American Educational Research Association, Seattle, WA.

Herzog, S. (2005). Measuring determinants of student return vs. dropout/stopout vs. transfer: A first-to-second year analysis of new freshman. *Research in Higher Education, 46*(8), 883–928.

Hosmer, D. W., & Lemeshow, S. (2000). *Applied logistic regression* (2nd ed.). New York, NY: Wiley.

Hunter, M. S., & Linder, C. W. (2005). First-year seminars. In M. L. Upcraft, J. N. Gardner, B. O. Barefoot, & Associates (Eds.), *Challenging and supporting the first-year student: A handbook for improving the first year of college* (pp. 275–291). San Francisco, CA: Jossey-Bass.

Kanoy, K. W., & Bruhn, J. W. (1996). Effects of a first-year living and learning residence hall on retention and academic performance. *Journal of the Freshman Year and Students in Transition, 8*(1), 7–23.

Kuh, G. D. (2008). *High-impact educational practices: What are they, who has access to them, and why they matter.* Washington, DC: Association of American Colleges and Universities.

McLachlan, G. J., & Krishnan, T. (1997). *The EM algorithm and extensions.* New York, NY: Wiley.

Nora, A., Barlow, E., & Crisp, G. (2005). Student persistence and degree attainment beyond the first year of college: The need for research. In A. Seidman (Ed.), *College student retention: Formula for student success* (pp. 129–154). West Port, CT: Prager Publishers.

Nora, A., Cabrera, A., Hagedorn, L. S., & Pascarella, E. (1996). Differential impacts of academic and social experiences on college-related behavioral outcomes across different ethnic and gender groups at four-year institutions. *Research in Higher Education, 37*(4), 427–451.

Pascarella, E. T., & Terenzini, P. T. (2005). *How college affects students: A third decade of research.* San Francisco, CA: Jossey-Bass.

Peterson, T. (1985). A comment on presenting results for logit and probit models. *American Sociological Review, 50*(1), 130–131.

Pike, G. R., Hansen, M. J., & Lin, C. H. (2011). Using instrumental variables to account for selection effects in research on first-year programs. *Research in Higher Education, 52*(1), 194–214.

Pike, G. R., Schroeder, C. C., & Berry, T. R. (1997). Enhancing the educational impact of residence halls: The relationship between residential learning communities and the first-year college experience and persistence. *Journal of College Student Development, 38,* 659–685.

Porter, S. R., & Swing, R. L. (2006). Understanding how first-year seminars affect persistence. *Research in Higher Education, 47*(1), 89–108.

Rocconi, L. M. (2011). The impact of learning communities on first year students' growth and development in college. *Research in Higher Education, 52*(1), 178–193.

Schnell, C. A., & Doetkott, C. D. (2003). First-year seminars produce long-term impact. *Journal of College Student Retention, 4*(4), 377–391.

Sharkness, J., DeAngelo, L., & Pryor, J. (2010). *CIRP Constructs technical report.* Los Angeles, CA: Higher Education Reseach Institue, UCLA. Retrieved from http://www.heri.ucla.edu/PDFs/technicalreport.pdf

Strumph, G., & Hunt, P. (1993). The effects of an orientation course on the retention and academic standing of entering freshmen, controlling for the volunteer effect. *Journal of the Freshman Year Experience, 5*, 7–14.

Tinto, V. (1975). Dropout from higher education: A theoretical synthesis of recent research. *Review of Educational Research, 45*, 89–125.

Tinto, V. (1987). *Leaving college: Rethinking the causes and cures of student attrition* (1st ed.). Chicago, IL: The University of Chicago Press.

Tinto, V. (1993). *Leaving college: Rethinking the causes and cures of student attrition* (2nd ed.). Chicago, IL: The University of Chicago Press.

Tinto, V. (1996). Reconstructing the first year of college. *Planning for Higher Education, 25*, 1–6.

Tinto, V. (1997). Classrooms as communities: Exploring the educational character of student persistence. *Journal of Higher Education, 68*, 599–623.

Upcraft, M. L., Gardner, J. N., & Barefoot, B. O. (2005). Principles of good practice of the first college year and summary of recommendations. In M. L. Upcraft, J. N. Gardner, B. O. Barefoot, & Associates (Eds.), *Challenging and supporting the first-year student: A handbook for improving the first year of college* (pp. 515–524). San Francisco, CA: Jossey-Bass.

Upcraft, M. L., Gardner, J. N., Barefoot, B. O., & Associates. (2005). *Challenging and supporting the first-year student: A handbook for improving the first year of college.* San Francisco, CA: Jossey-Bass.

Wolfe, J. (1993). Institutional integration, academic success and persistence of first-year commuter and resident students. *Journal of College Student Development, 34*, 321–326.

Zeller, W. J. (2005). First-year student living environments. In M. L. Upcraft, J. N. Gardner, B. O. Barefoot, & Associates (Eds.), *Challenging and supporting the first-year student: A handbook for improving the first year of college* (pp. 410–427). San Francisco, CA: Jossey-Bass.

LINDA DEANGELO *is an assistant professor of higher education in the Department of Administrative and Policy Studies at the University of Pittsburgh.*

Appendix 4.1. Description of Variables and Measures

Variables	Scale
Dependent variable	
Intent to reenroll at current institution	0 = no, 1 = yes
Independent variables	
Control variables	
Student background characteristics	
Gender: female	1 = no, 2 = yes
First-generation student: Yes	1 = no, 2 = yes
SAT comprehensive score	Continuous
Retention risk entering freshman	
Concern with financing college (Reference group: none)	
Some	1 = no, 2 = yes
Major	1 = no, 2 = yes
Need extra time to degree	1 = no, 2 = yes
Transfer to different institution	1 = no, 2 = yes
Institution attended	
Institution type: private	1 = no, 2 = yes
Institutional selectivity	Continuous
Study variables	
Classroom experiences	
Ease of academic adjustment	Continuous—A construct measure that includes four variables assessing success at what your professors expect of you academically, developing effective study skills, adjusting to the academic demands of college, and managing time effectively. Each of the variables is on a three-point scale: 1 = unsuccessful to 3 = completely successful.
"Habits of mind" for student success	Continuous—A construct measure that includes 11 variables assessing the frequency of asking questions in class, supporting opinions with a logical argument, seeking solutions to problems and explaining them to others, revising papers to improve writing, evaluating the quality and reliability of information, taking a risk because you have more to gain, seeking alternative solutions to a problem, looking up scientific research articles and resources, exploring topics on your own, even though it was not required for class, accepting mistakes as part of the learning process, and seeking feedback on your academic work. Each of the variables is on a three-point scale: 1 = not at all to 3 = frequently.

(Continued)

Appendix 4.1. Continued

Variables	Scale
Academic disengagement	Continuous—A construct measure that includes five variables assessing the frequency of coming late to class, falling asleep in class, turning in course assignments late, turning in course assignments that did not reflect best work, and skipping class. Each of the variables is on a three-point scale: $1 =$ not at all to $3 =$ frequently.
Community service as part of class	
(Reference group: not at all)	
Occasionally	$1 =$ no, $2 =$ yes
Frequently	$1 =$ no, $2 =$ yes
Learning community/linked courses	$1 =$ no, $2 =$ yes
First-year seminar: college adjustment	$1 =$ no, $2 =$ yes
Experiences outside of the classroom	
Discussed course content with students	
(Reference group: not at all)	
Occasionally	$1 =$ no, $2 =$ yes
Frequently	$1 =$ no, $2 =$ yes
Studied with other students	
(Reference group: not at all)	
Occasionally	$1 =$ no, $2 =$ yes
Frequently	$1 =$ no, $2 =$ yes
Worked on professor's research project	
(Reference group: not at all)	
Occasionally	$1 =$ no, $2 =$ yes
Frequently	$1 =$ no, $2 =$ yes
Had meaningful and honest discussions about race/ethnic relations outside of class with students from a racial/ethnic group other than your own	$1 =$ never to $5 =$ very often

(Continued)

Appendix 4.1. Continued

Variables	Scale
Had intellectual discussions outside of class with students from a racial/ethnic group other than your own	1 = never to 5 = very often
Student–faculty interaction	Continuous—A construct measure that includes six variables assessing if you have meet with faculty during office hours or communicated regularly with faculty. Both measured on a two-point scale: 1 = no, 2 = yes. If you have received advice or educational guidance about your educational program from professors and asked professors for advice after class. Both measured on a three-point scale: 1= not at all to 3 = frequently, the amount of contact you have had with faculty outside of office hours. Measured 1 = never to 6 = daily, and satisfaction with the amount of contact with faculty. Measured 1 = can't rate/no experience to 6 = very satisfied.
First-year academic achievement	
College GPA	1 = C– or less (below 1.75) to 6 = A (3.75–4.0)
Retention risk at the end of first year	
Concern with financing college (Reference group: none)	
Some	1 = no, 2 = yes
Major	1 = no, 2 = yes

Appendix 4.2. Logistic Regression Coefficients in the Blocked and Final Model

	Model 1	Model 2	Model 3	Model 4	Model 5	Final Model
Control variables						
Background						
Gender: female	−0.154	−0.144	−0.180	−0.239*	−0.251*	0.266
First generation: yes	−0.217	−0.249	−0.251	−0.222	−0.239	−0.223
Parental income	−0.037*	−0.033	−0.034	−0.029	−0.037	−0.036
SAT comprehensive score	0.01**	0.001***	0.001***	0.001***	0.001	0.001
Retention risk entering freshman						
Financial concern (Reference group: none)						
Some	0.034	0.037	0.052	0.043	0.079	0.052
Major	−0.334	−0.314	−0.298	−0.300	−0.010	−0.040
Likely need extra time to degree	0.170*	0.168*	0.178*	0.161*	0.160*	0.169*
Likely transfer to different institution	−0.633***	−0.644***	−0.637***	−0.638***	−0.646***	−0.646***
Institution attended						
Institutional type: private	−0.221**	−0.180*	−0.219**	−0.312***	−0.298**	−0.291**
Institutional selectivity	0.002***	0.002***	0.002***	0.002***	0.002***	0.002***
Study variables						
Residence and employment						
First-year housing (Reference group: first year/special interest)						
Regular student housing		−0.076	−0.064	−0.012	−0.021	0.999**
Off-campus housing		0.532**	0.535**	0.687**	0.661**	1.326*
Worked full-time first year		−0.409**	−0.436**	−0.431**	−0.367*	−0.340*
First-year classroom engagement						
Ease of academic adjustment			−0.003	−0.005	−0.013*	−0.014*
Habits of mind for student success			0.015*	−0.013	−0.013	−0.012
Academic disengagement			−0.017**	−0.019**	−0.013*	−0.012
Service learning (Reference group: not at all)						
Occasionally			0.178	0.103	0.074	0.087
Frequently			0.527*	0.317	0.333	0.355

(Continued)

Appendix 4.2. Continued

	Model 1	Model 2	Model 3	Model 4	Model 5	Final Model
Learning community: yes			−0.028	−0.101	−0.116	−0.116
First-year seminar: yes			0.045	−0.017	−0.020	−0.819*
Engagement outside of the classroom						
Discuss course content with students (Reference group: not at all)						
Occasionally				0.708***	0.691***	1.341**
Frequently				0.866***	0.842***	1.571**
Studied with other students (Reference group: not at all)						
Occasionally				0.167	0.176	0.184
Frequently				0.412*	0.425*	0.420*
Worked on professor's research project (Reference group: not at all)						
Occasionally				−0.290**	−0.270*	−0.287**
Frequently				0.060	0.055	0.053
Had with other racial/ethnic groups						
Meaningful discussions about race				0.087	0.092	0.093
Meaningful intellectual discussions			0.096	0.107*	0.111*	
Student–faculty interaction				0.031***	0.029***	0.028***
First-year academic achievement						
College GPA					0.154**	0.160**
Retention risk at the end of first year						
Financial concern (Reference group: none)						
Some					0.074	0.098
Major					−0.496**	−0.489**

(Continued)

Appendix 4.2. Continued

	Model 1	Model 2	Model 3	Model 4	Model 5	Final Model
Interaction terms						
Gender and discussing course content with students outside of class (Reference group: male and not at all)						
Female and occasionally						−0.644
Female and frequently						−0.442
Housing and discussing course content with students outside of class (Reference group: first year/special interest and not at all)						
Regular and occasionally						−1.048***
Regular and frequently						−1.175***
Off-campus and occasionally						−0.347
Off-campus and frequently						−1.258*
First-year seminar and discussing course content with students outside of class (Reference group: no and not at all)						
Yes and occasionally						0.873*
Yes and frequently						0.860*
AIC	432782.7	430084.2	427139.8	416669.5	413070.9	410174.1
BIC	432871.8	430197.7	427310.0	416912.6	413338.4	410506.3
Degrees of freedom	11	14	21	30	33	41

$N = 24,443$. Data have been weighted to represent the national sample of first-time, full-time freshmen who retained through year one.
$^*p < .05.$ $^{**}p < .01.$ $^{***}p < .001.$

5

This chapter will examine characteristics of first-year experience programs in community colleges, with specific attention to the extant research about their effectiveness, the ways in which research and program delivery can be integrated, and the unique challenges of delivering FYE programs and conducting research about them in community colleges.

The First-Year Experience in Community Colleges

Trudy Bers, Donna Younger

Introduction

Community colleges enroll 42% of first-time freshmen in postsecondary education (American Association of Community Colleges, 2014), but until recently have received little attention for their first-year experience (FYE) programs. Programs and services addressing the needs of new students were introduced in four-year institutions and later appeared in community colleges that learned from the experiences of the senior institutions. Similarly, research and funding to encourage and support first-year programs came later to community colleges. Despite the relative youth of FYE programs in community colleges, they are growing both in number and scope (Bailey & Alfonso, 2005) and are stimulating attention in the literature and by conference offerings as professionals work to improve student persistence and success through FYE programs.

The purpose of this chapter is to examine characteristics of FYE programs in community colleges, with specific attention to research about their contributions to student success. We will also identify strategies for integrating research and program delivery and for using data to improve programs. Finally, we will identify unique challenges of delivering FYE programs and conducting research about them in community colleges.

NEW DIRECTIONS FOR INSTITUTIONAL RESEARCH, no. 160 © 2014 Wiley Periodicals, Inc.
Published online in Wiley Online Library (wileyonlinelibrary.com) • DOI: 10.1002/ir.20062

Characteristics of First-Year Experience Programs and the Extant Research

Although there is no standard definition of an FYE program, there are a variety of services and practices commonly associated with FYE that address students' academic and transitional needs in both two-year and four-year institutions. The emergence of FYE led to the development of new approaches and services across time, and in many cases the systems and policies that support them followed later. The first-year seminar implemented at the University of South Carolina in 1972 identified needs and issues related to the support and retention of entering college students (University 101, 2010).

With the new emphasis on entering students reflected in seminar design and content, efforts to improve in areas such as orientation, advising, and early alert quickly followed and were associated with the principles of FYE. Beyond improvements in student services, emphasis on classroom practices that depended on the active involvement of students also emerged, including such approaches as common reading programs, learning communities, service learning, and problem-based learning (Upcraft, Gardner, Barefoot, & Associates, 2005).

Yet another area that requires mention is that of developmental or remedial education. Not an FYE program specifically, developmental education is an overriding and substantial issue for a majority of community college students, and one that many encounter in their first year even if their institutions do not require them to register for those courses upon entry. In this chapter, we purposely do not discuss developmental education, crucial as it is, because developmental education requires a separate presentation of its own and would divert us from addressing core and emerging elements of the FYE.

Research on the impact of FYE has typically reflected institutional experiences and findings and has been less focused on broad-based research that generalizes about FYE as an approach to higher education. In the thirty years since the introduction of FYE as an organizing principle of higher education, institutions and organizations have devoted effort to developing and implementing practices and conducting research to evaluate their impact in ways meaningful at the campus level rather than to the wider postsecondary community. Centers such as the National Resource Center for The First-Year Experience and Students in Transition, the Indiana University Center for Postsecondary Education, the Higher Education Research Institute at the University of California, Los Angeles, and initiatives to change approaches to students such as Achieving the Dream (AtD) and the Foundations of Excellence® have in recent years done more to identify elements of FYE programs that support student success and retention. They base much of their work on national data drawn from multiple institutions. A recent summary of Opening Doors programs examined the impact of several approaches to fostering student achievement: financial incentives, learning communities, enhanced academic counseling, and enhanced target services (Scrivener & Coghlan, 2011). Using random assignments, their research showed these interventions held promise but were not uniformly and consistently effective. Karp (2011) provided another publication that examined nonacademic supports for students. She noted that positive student outcomes were achieved in programs that involved creating social relationships, clarifying aspirations and enhancing commitment, developing college know-how, and making college feasible.

Scholarship and professional development related to FYE identify several services as primary elements of FYE programs and indicate a frequent overlap between FYE programs and those targeted to underprepared and first-generation students who often need strong support services to succeed in college. Although the development of FYE programs has been associated primarily with four-year institutions, in the past fifteen years or so, community colleges and other two-year institutions have done much to adapt the core elements of FYE to their populations and structures, based largely on research that highlights distinctions between the two types of institutions. For example, FYE components that are typically implemented as requirements in four-year institutions (such as Orientation) are more often offered as options and in a briefer format than at senior institutions. The nature of the more transient community college population has prompted the adjustment in structure and policy regarding orientation. We wish we could clearly differentiate FYE elements unique to community colleges, but in reality, many two- and four-year institutions share common interventions. Indeed, we contend that open-enrollment, commuter universities with large numbers of part-time students have more in common with community colleges than with more selective, residential universities. But that is a different study.

Despite the commonality in FYE approaches between two-year and four-year schools, it is important for institutional researchers at community colleges to focus on what is known about their effectiveness at community colleges. Quite simply, community college personnel are more likely to learn from and pay attention to the literature about FYE programs in community colleges because often they assume what occurs at four-year institutions has limited relevance to their domain. The descriptions of core FYE elements that follow reveal that the FYE seminar within community colleges has been more widely researched than other FYE practices. They also reveal the difficulty in drawing data-based conclusions about the effectiveness of these services in supporting student retention and success.

Core Components of FYE Programs

A number of programs and services within community colleges provide students additional support both within and outside the classroom. The

Table 5.1. Comparing First-Year Seminars in Two-Year and Four-Year Institutions (Percent of Institutions)

	Two-Year	Four-Year
Seminar types		
Extended orientation	76.5	57.9
Academic seminars	29.0	53.8
Preprofessional	12.2	14.9
Basic study skills	41.3	21.6
Other	14.8	24.7
Academic credit		
1 credit	41.8	42.5
3 credits	34.2	32.7
Required for		
All first year	21.5	46.0
Some	48.8	34.6
None	29.8	19.4

Source: Tobolowsky, B. F. (2008). *2006 National Survey of First-Year Seminars: Continuing innovations in the collegiate curriculum*. The First-Year Experience Monograph Series No. 51. Columbia: National Resource Center for The First-Year Experience and Students in Transition, University of South Carolina.

following core components are supported by decades of college impact research and vetted practices.

First-Year Seminars. The seminar provides a forum, typically in the first term, for new students to examine their entry to college and the implications it has for their identity, their time, and their intellectual growth. Seminars are offered in a myriad of formats (preterm immersion, standard class schedule, retreats); are known by various names (e.g., FYE 101, Success Seminar); and are taught by varying combinations of faculty, staff, and administrators.

Of the 968 institutions responding to the 2006 National Survey on First-Year Seminars (Tobolowsky, 2008), 821 reported that their institutions offer the seminar and of these 196 were community colleges (24%). As shown in Table 5.1, survey results reveal distinctions between institutional types with respect to the seminar. The differences in seminar type reflect differences in student populations, with community colleges focusing more on basic skills and transition to college, given their higher enrollments of underprepared and first-generation students. Also, community colleges that require the seminar of some but not all students often require it for students who place into developmental courses. In general, community colleges tend to develop the seminar to fill skill and knowledge gaps while four-year institutions are somewhat more likely to focus on students' entry into the academic community. Data from this study are descriptive and provide little to permit assessing the association of first-year seminars with students' success. However, the more striking difference concerns the role of the seminar as mandatory or optional. Four-year institutions are

NEW DIRECTIONS FOR INSTITUTIONAL RESEARCH • DOI: 10.1002/ir

significantly more likely to require the seminar of all students (46%) than community colleges (22%). Community colleges are more likely to require the seminar for no students (30%) than senior institutions (19%). Community colleges are most likely to require the seminar for some students (49%) and this category shows the most rapid growth (32% in the 2003 survey).

Studies providing empirical evidence about the association between first-year experience or college success seminars and student attainment are sparse. Much of what does exist is institution-specific, though several multi-institution studies have generalized that the seminar has positive impact on retention and student performance (Cho & Karp, 2012), academic progress (Tobolowsky, Cox, & Wagner, 2005), and intention to persist (Porter & Swing, 2006). In their synthesis of research that addresses the impact of college on students, Pascarella and Terenzini (2005) conclude that:

> In short, the weight of evidence indicates that FYS [first year seminar] participation has statistically significant and substantial, positive effects on students' successful transition to college and the likelihood of persistence into the second year as well as on academic performance while in college on a considerable array of other college experiences known to be related directly and indirectly to bachelor's degree completion. (p. 403)

Although none of this research addresses first-year seminars in the community college specifically, studies of community college seminars are beginning to appear. Zeidenberg, Jenkins, and Calcagno (2007) report on a study that tracked Florida students for 17 semesters, beginning with fall 1999. After controlling for student characteristics, they found that students enrolled in a Student Life Skills (SLS) course were 8% more likely to earn a credential than nonenrollees. They also found that for students who did not take remediation, SLS enrollment was associated with a 9% increase in the chances of completion, and for students who did take remediation, SLS enrollment was associated with a 5% increase in the chances of completion.

Other studies focusing on community college seminars revealed that seminar participants earned higher grade point averages (Wahlstrom, 1993) and earned more credits than nonparticipants (Stupka, 1993).

Further, Miller, Janz, and Chen (2007) found that all students, regardless of academic ability prior to college, benefited from the seminar in terms of persistence and credits earned.

Learning Communities.   Although there are variations in structure and delivery, learning communities depend on linking two or more courses to emphasize connections among bodies of knowledge and to create a cohort of students with shared experiences. The Community College Research Center (CCRC) found that of the four areas of community colleges that were studied (learning communities, developmental education, student services, and college-wide reform), learning communities yielded the most significant evidence of positive impact on persistence (Bailey & Alfonso,

2005). Recently, six community colleges participated in the National Center for Postsecondary Research's Learning Communities Demonstration. The purpose of this demonstration is to determine whether learning communities are effective in helping students succeed in developmental education. Using a random assignment methodology to examine learning communities at Hillsborough Community College in Florida, researchers concluded "Overall (for the full study sample), Hillsborough's learning communities program did not have a meaningful impact on students' academic success" although there was some evidence the program had positive impacts on some educational outcomes for the third cohort of students in the study (Weiss, Visher, & Wathington, 2010, p. ES-3).

Another random assignment study of community college learning communities was conducted at Kingsborough Community College. Researchers found that compared to students in the control group students in the learning communities felt more engaged and integrated into the college community; had better educational outcomes initially, but the effects diminished over time; and moved more quickly through developmental English. Researchers found mixed evidence as to the effect of learning communities on persistence (Scrivener et al., 2008).

Research from individual institutions is less visible, probably in part because many describe rather than evaluate their learning communities, and in part because they do not publish or present empirical data that show no association between learning communities and student achievement. This does not suggest that assessment is not happening; rather, institutional studies are often done for the institution and not for a broader audience.

Even if learning communities were shown to be an effective strategy for improving student attainment, colleges have encountered persistent challenges in bringing them to scale. Challenges include the cost of communities where faculty are compensated and/or have adjusted teaching loads; difficulties in recruiting students into learning communities, a barrier encountered in a number of institutions of all sizes; and integrating course material so the community is seen by students as seamless rather than composed of different courses that happen to meet consecutively.

Currently, enthusiasm for learning communities remains high, but the reality for many community colleges is that their value is unproven and they affect relatively few students.

Orientation.   Across postsecondary institutions, orientation for new students varies in terms of length, content, and involvement of faculty and staff in academic affairs and student affairs. While there is little research that assesses the impact of orientation on student success, findings from two descriptive studies are particularly interesting in relation to each other. In the first "comprehensive national survey of the first year," The Policy Center on the First Year of College found that two-year colleges typically limited orientation to a half day and did not require attendance, while most four-year institutions required participation in orientation that was two days or more in length (Upcraft et al., 2005). The tendencies of two-year institutions are clearly related to the great numbers of part-time and nonresidential students whose time on campus is limited. The impact of this phenomenon, albeit indirectly, is addressed by Reason, Cox, McIntosh, and Terenzini (2010) in a three-year study of four-year institutions that addressed the relationship between learning outcomes and student engagement in Documenting Effective Educational Practices (DEEP) learning experiences. Findings revealed that the length, structure, and involvement of family in orientation had significant correlations to student engagement.

The observation that "longer is better" with respect to orientation can be extracted as a lesson for both two-year and four-year institutions (Gardner & Barefoot, 2011). Given the nature of community colleges as open enrollment institutions serving many nonresidential, part-time students, the obstacles to "longer" orientation required for new students are daunting. Research assessing the impact of orientation on the success, development, and retention of new students is essential to encourage institutions to dedicate the resources and changes necessary for making orientation both substantial and mandatory.

Early Alert Systems.   These systems facilitate timely response to student problems immediately when they become evident. They depend on early assessment of student learning within the course, faculty participation in the early alert system, and response by support services directly related to the problems of individual students. Observable behaviors that trigger an early alert may include never attending class but remaining on the roster, excessive absences, excessive tardiness, academic concerns such as failure to turn in assignments, low homework/quiz scores, low test scores, and personal concerns revealed to or suspected by the instructor.

Because early alert addresses personal as well as academic difficulties, a number of units within the institution may be involved, including advising, academic support, and financial aid. This design recognizes the importance of looking beyond symptoms to causes and the fact that both social/personal difficulties and academic skill deficiencies may interact and contribute to problems students have in their classes (Lotkowski, Robbins, & Noeth, 2004). Increasingly, software enables connections among the services responding to the early alert system and may be linked to other information management systems within the institution. Most community colleges that use software applications rely on homegrown rather than commercial products (Hobsons, 2008).

Research about the impact of early alert systems at community colleges remains slim. Sinclair Community College reported at-risk students in an early alert system had higher persistence rates than non-at-risk students in the general population (Price, 2010), and Chappell (2010) reported that successful outcomes in Frederick Community College courses rose from 52% to 66% since the fall 2008 installation of an early alert system for all courses. Other institution-specific reports also indicate systems appear to

NEW DIRECTIONS FOR INSTITUTIONAL RESEARCH • DOI: 10.1002/ir

make a difference. As with other FYE components, challenges of funding, sustaining faculty involvement, and providing immediate services to identified students can make it difficult to implement an effective early alert system.

Academic Advising.   While academic advising is considered an important service provided for students, it is a key component of FYE programs in community college because of its role as a clearinghouse for student needs and problems and in referring students for assistance to other more specialized units. Structurally, advising may be organized around centralized models that typically rely on nonfaculty advisors or decentralized models that involve faculty advising majors within the discipline or those exploring the discipline. Most community colleges (75%) use a centralized advising center model and "strongly encourage" students to choose a major (Upcraft et al., 2005).

The intake model of advising common to community colleges relies on a relatively small advising staff and may appear to have limited opportunities to have direct impact on student success. A study of six California community colleges indicated that coordinated services of academic support and advising had greater impact on student success than either of the services provided independently of the other. When working to improve the academic standing of probation students, the coordinated services led to a higher number of credits earned and increases in GPA than the stand-alone services (Scrivener, Sommo, & Collado, 2009). Two Ohio community colleges used enhanced academic counseling approaches that included stipends, multiple meetings with an assigned counselor, and a smaller number of students to each counselor. Researchers found that the program had modest positive effects while students were in the program but effects were not sustained beyond that time (Scrivener & Coghlan, 2011). Several AtD community colleges (see below) have adopted a case management approach to advising. For example, South Texas College found that students in the case management approach had higher rates of successful course completion, grades of A, B, or C, persistence from term to term, and graduation than other students at the college (South Texas College, 2006).

Three special challenges in implementing effective advising programs in community colleges are the ever-present budget constraints that limit the number of advisors and technical support available to them; complexity of providing accurate information to students who are unsure of their majors and unsure where they wish to transfer; and propensity of students to self-advise or rely on peers rather than to seek assistance from trained personnel. To make community colleges accessible, many institutions have been reluctant to impose what some see as "barriers" to students, with seeing an advisor being one such hypothetical barrier.

Student Engagement and Student Success.   As FYE programs have developed, additional practices have emerged that strengthen student engagement and thereby support student success and retention goals. These practices include common reading programs, service learning, and mentoring. Of these, service learning has yielded the most research examining its impact on student success. A recent study by the American Association of Community Colleges (AACC) examined the impact of service learning on learning outcomes at 13 community colleges participating in the Horizons service learning grant project. After controlling for pre–service learning, academic progress, and activities within the target courses beyond service learning, the study found that service learning indicates greater student outcomes in five of six learning outcomes, with teamwork and career skills yielding the highest scores. This is consistent with previous studies of Horizons institutions, but AACC recommends further research to examine more closely the specific skills and knowledge acquired that relate most directly to academic success (Prentice & Robinson, 2010).

Practices designed to increase student engagement are predicated on the suggestion that engagement leads to greater levels of student success and persistence (Pascarella & Terenzini, 2005). However, recent research that examined the theoretical basis for research associating engagement and student success indicates there are significant differences in relevance of the theory for two- and four-year institutions (Marti, 2008). The finding that elements of engagement such as student involvement, student efforts, and institutional environment are related to success and persistence was derived from research at four-year institutions and is more applicable to their students. To more accurately determine the impact of engagement strategies, both in and out of the classroom, on student success additional research is needed to examine the nature of social and academic integration at two-year institutions (Marti, 2008).

National Initiatives

In 2004, the Lumina Foundation for Education funded AtD, a national initiative to improve community college student success. While not explicitly focused on the first year, four of the five AtD performance indicators (successfully complete courses, advance from remedial to credit-bearing courses, enroll in and successfully complete gatekeeper courses, and enroll from one semester to the next) clearly apply to first years as well as other students. Indeed, if students do not meet these goals as freshmen they simply will not be successful in earning degrees/certificates or transferring. A year later the Gardner Institute launched its Foundations of Excellence® program for two-year colleges. The program is premised on Foundational Dimensions that provide a model for evaluating and improving the experience of new students. And in 2006 the Community College Survey of Student Engagement (CCSSE) added a Survey of Entering Student Engagement (SENSE) to its tools. The SENSE elicits the perceptions of new students about their experiences at and engagements within the institution during

NEW DIRECTIONS FOR INSTITUTIONAL RESEARCH • DOI: 10.1002/ir

the first weeks of the term and is intended to help colleges improve the programs and services targeted to new students in order to improve persistence and graduation rates.

The Foundations of Excellence® and AtD share an emphasis on collecting, interpreting, and using data to enhance the understanding of student achievement, barriers to success, and program effectiveness, while the SENSE is a vehicle for collecting data about new students to inform institutional discussions and improvement efforts. We cite these three projects because they illustrate growing attention by community colleges to the experience of first-year students and increased funding by foundations to support community colleges' work. Foundations have provided substantial support for all three programs, especially AtD, which has received more than $100 million from more than 15 different funders.

Strategies for Integrating Research and Program Delivery and Using Data

Institutional researchers and individuals who plan and deliver FYE programs often come from quite different perspectives with respect to compiling and using data measuring program effectiveness. Institutional research professionals are accustomed to identifying research questions, determining the data needed to conduct the research, creating processes for gathering and storing the data, and analyzing the data. Institutional research professionals should also be familiar with ways to present the data beyond comprehensive tables with multidecimal frequencies and percentages. Alternative presentation approaches include figures, graphs, bullet points of key findings, and even photographs or cartoons to illustrate major points.

Individuals who plan and deliver FYE programs frequently come from different perspectives. Many are housed in student affairs or academic support service departments. They are passionate in their desire to help students, enthusiastic about what they do, and may believe that because their intentions are so good and they have heard about direct measures of successful interventions, program outcomes must be positive. They may also be more comfortable with and knowledgeable about performance indicators that measure use ("how many") and satisfaction rather than the attainment of specific learning or behavioral outcomes. And they are probably more focused on the logistics of program implementation and working directly with students than conceptualizing and undertaking the data-gathering tasks essential for research.

We acknowledge that not all community colleges, especially smaller institutions, have institutional research offices and in many cases the office is severely underfunded and short staffed (Morest & Jenkins, 2007). Thus, faculty or staff members may be assigned tasks without having any actual training in institutional or social science research. While we refer to institutional research in the strategies presented below, you should expand its definition to include all staff assigned institutional research functions even if they are not housed in or carry the title of Institutional Researcher.

Our strategies to integrate research and program delivery and to use data to improve programs are based on our premise that institutional research professionals and service providers come from the different perspectives noted above. Each group brings talents and interests to the table and needs to inform the other.

Meet Early and Periodically. It is important for institutional research professionals and program planners/deliverers to meet together when a particular service is first being considered and/or revised. It is much more difficult if not impossible to create research questions and gather data about program outcomes after the fact. It is also important for meetings to occur periodically while a program is underway, though such meetings may occur electronically or informally. These "meetings" should ensure that appropriate data gathering is taking place and whether modifications in research questions or data gathering should be made.

Specify Program Objectives. It is imperative that intended program outcomes be clearly and explicitly stated, preferably with quantitative outcome objectives such as "80 percent of program participants will return to the College for the next semester" or "75 percent of program participants will improve their self-confidence as indicated by pre- and post-test results on an institutional self-confidence survey." Program deliverers may find it challenging—even threatening—to be this explicit, and the institution may not have a culture where being so precise is the norm. To use quantitative objectives it is imperative that service providers participate in setting them, know the consequences if objectives are not met, and have adequate support so their programs have the chance to succeed. In the next section, we will devote more space to research issues such as determining whether or not an intervention was the reason for student success (or failure).

Identify Data. Once program objectives are clarified, then institutional research professionals and service deliverers need to determine what data to collect to be able to evaluate the program's effectiveness. It may be helpful for those unaccustomed to thinking about data to consider them in three broad categories: student attributes, FYE services, and outcomes.

Student Attributes. Student attributes are those student characteristics that enable us to assess differential participation in and outcomes of FYE programs by subgroups, including but not limited to disaggregating into developmental/college level, gender, age, race/ethnicity, full-time/part-time, and other subgroups. Most attribute data will come from the institution's student information system, but some relevant and potentially powerful explanatory variables may come from other data sources or, sadly, not be available. For example, few colleges collect updated data about students' employment or whether or not they are responsible for children or other household members.

FYE Services.   Each institution can identify the FYE and related services it wants to examine. Data to be collected on each service include whether or not the student participated, which may be a simple yes or no, and the frequency of participation for services such as mentoring or tutoring, where students may participate multiple times. Creating data collection processes and entering data into electronic files may be new efforts for service providers, especially if they see these as barriers to student participation or nuisance tasks taking way valuable time from working directly with students.

Outcomes.   Outcome data may be derived from the student information management system, for example, grades in courses; updated placements in reading, writing, or math; enrollment in subsequent terms; and academic status such as good standing or probation. The benefit of using such data to measure outcomes is that data are widely understood and collected as part of the institution's regular business operations. Other outcome data may be more elusive. For example, improved self-confidence—as measured on an institutionally developed survey—may be difficult to assess because the researcher must account for valid survey item construction, approximate the appropriate time to administer the survey, and identify which student sample will represent the overall population.

Assign Responsibility for Collecting and Storing Data.   As simple as this sounds, departments whose focus is on serving students may not think to explicitly assign responsibility for collecting, entering, and/or storing data to staff. While sometimes it is possible to go back and recapture data, when it comes to tracking the times students come for services, the specific services they seek from a multifaceted student support office, and even their identifications is often difficult if not impossible. Helping staff to understand the reason for taking on this responsibility and the importance of it may help to improve implementation and accuracy.

Agree on Data Analyses.   In the real world of community college program implementation and evaluation, institutions rarely have the option to conduct rigorous research using such approaches as random assignment, matched comparisons, propensity score methods, or interrupted time-series designs (Brock, 2010; Padgett, Salisbury, An, & Pascarella, 2010). Those unfamiliar with statistics often ask whether results of empirical studies were statistically significant, not realizing that results may have little or no substantive or practical significance even if they are statistically significant, or that when a study includes all students in a population tests of statistical significance are inappropriate. They frequently confuse association/correlation with causation, believing that if two or more variables move together, one causes the other. While our intention is not to argue against using sophisticated statistics to examine the association between FYE programs and student outcomes, we caution against relying on them for several reasons. They may not be possible to use, may provide little practical information to guide decision making, and may dissuade service providers from being willing to incorporate even simple frequency counts or cross-tabulations into their program evaluations.

Present Data and Information Clearly and Simply. This admonition is directed to any practitioner providing research data about FYE programs and services, from the simplest counts of usage to advanced statistical analyses of their impacts. We suggest the beginning point is to ask three simple questions: what is the story, to whom is it being told, and what actions are desired as a result of their knowing the story? The answers to these questions may not be so simple, but they are worth the time to consider and they can then influence how the data and information are presented. For example, some audiences prefer long reports to give credibility to research; in these cases, we urge you to include a short executive summary as well. Some audiences want PowerPoints with short bulleted lists and multicolor charts, while others want narrative briefs that may include some charts. Desired actions may include continuing support for a program, revising a program, changing policies such as making what had previously been an optional program mandatory, taking a small program to scale, and more. The point is, while data and information must be accurate, they can also be presented in a manner that helps leaders use them to inform decisions.

Collaborate, Collaborate, Collaborate. Our final strategy is one that actually threads through all the specific suggestions noted above. To integrate program delivery and research, and to use data to improve programs, it is essential that program deliverers feel a part of the research process and a sense of ownership of the results. Absent this, they are likely to reject research as inaccurate, irrelevant, or an impediment to delivering their services. Institutional research professionals may balk at having to explain research methodologies to FYE program personnel, and FYE personnel in turn may wonder why they have to take time away from their students to deal with research. But if both institutional research professionals and FYE personnel commit to the overarching goal of improving FYE programs and fostering student success, both are likely to be more willing to work together.

Challenges of Delivering and Conducting Research

We have alluded to a number of challenges of conducting research about FYE programs in community colleges in the section above, including the different talents and priorities between those who deliver and those who research FYE programs, not bringing research questions into the conversation when programs are first designed and implemented, agreeing on appropriate research questions including clarifying intended program outcomes, implementing the mechanics of research such as collecting and storing data, and presenting findings in ways that foster understanding and use of those results.

In this section, we concentrate specifically on the characteristics of two-year colleges and our students to highlight additional challenges. We hasten to add that some four-year institutions will have the same challenges. In addition, many of the characteristics noted below are overlapping and re-inforcing.

Transient Student Populations.   Many community college students are transient, leaving their institutions within one year of entry. For exam-ple, data from 113 community colleges in 18 states participating in AtD show that only 48% of credential-seeking students new to the institutions in the fall persisted to the next fall and only 34% enrolled in any term in the third year (Lee, 2010). Students did not leave their institutions because they had completed programs or transferred; only 8% completed a creden-tial and 7% had transferred by the third year after entry. Many community college students also have stop-in/stop-out enrollment patterns, making it both conceptually and methodologically challenging to track their progress.

Part-Time Enrollment.   At least 60% of community colleges' 11.78 million students are enrolled part-time (AACC, 2011). Moreover, students who begin full-time do not continue as full-time students. Data from AtD institutions show that only 31% of students who began as full-time stu-dents remained full-time through the first year (Clery, 2010). Being part-time means students may have less commitment to the role of student, less likelihood of taking advantage of FYE and other support services, and less likelihood of being actively engaged at the institution. Data from the 2010 Community College Survey of Student Engagement show, for example, that the scores of full-time students on the five CCSSE benchmarks range from 5.1 to 9.3 points higher than scores of part-time students (J. F. Crumpley, personal communication, January 2011). CCSSE results also show differ-ences in the percent of full- and part-time students who have taken a study skills course (18% and 13%), participated in a college orientation program or course (32% and 23%), and participated in an organized learning com-munity of linked courses or study groups (11% and 7%; CCSSE, 2010).

Looking at part-time students and their participation at the college is partly a chicken and egg discussion: do part-time students have less time or flexibility to participate in FYE programs, or are FYE programs geared to full-time students who presumably have more on-campus time, at least in classes?

Conclusion

We have noted a variety of factors that make implementing and eval-uating FYE programs particularly challenging in community colleges. None present insurmountable obstacles, but taken together they present a formidable array of issues that must be addressed. Some reside in the characteristics of students—largely part-time and transient; some in the characteristics of employees—absence of research skills and a focus on implementation; and some in resource constraints.

President Obama has issued a call for community colleges to produce significantly more graduates than in the past, and obviously students who do not make it through their first year will not earn their degrees. Thus, first-year experience programs have never been so needed. And research to validate their impact, especially in community colleges, is also sorely needed to justify expenditures, to identify small programs that warrant bringing to scale, and to provide the evidence needed to terminate programs that are not working or that are simply too costly for the value they provide.

References

American Association of Community Colleges (AACC). (2011). *Fast facts*. Retrieved from http://www.aacc.nche.edu/AboutCC/Documents/Archive/FactSheet2011.pdf

American Association of Community Colleges (AACC). (2014). *Fast facts from our fact sheet*. Retrieved from http://www.aacc.nche.edu/AboutCC/Pages/fastfactsfactsheet.aspx

Bailey, T. R., & Alfonso, M. (2005). *Paths to persistence: An analysis of research on program effectiveness at community colleges*. New York, NY: Community College Research Center, Teachers College, Columbia University.

Brock, T. (2010). *Evaluating programs for community college students: How do we know what works?* New York, NY: MDRC.

Chappell, C. (2010, August). 'Early alert' systems send students warnings, advice. *Community College Times*. Retrieved from http://www.ccdaily.com/Pages/Campus-Issues/Early-alert-systems-send-students-warnings-advice.aspx

Cho, S. W., & Karp, M. M. (2012). *Student success courses and educational outcomes at Virginia community colleges* (CCRC Working Paper No. 40). New York, NY: Columbia University, Teachers College, Community College Research Center.

Clery, S. (2010). Attendance and completion patterns. *Data Notes: Keeping Informed About Achieving the Dream Data, 5*(2), 1–4.

Community College Survey of Student Engagement (CCSSE). (2010). *Standard breakout reports*. Retrieved from http://www.ccsse.org/survey/reports/2010/reports.cfm

Gardner, J. N., & Barefoot, B. O. (2011, February). *Best practice in the first college year: Defining what works and why*. Presentation at the Annual Conference of the First-Year Experience, Atlanta, GA.

Hobsons, T. (2008). *Hobsons survey of community colleges*. Cincinnati, OH: Author.

Karp, M. M. (2011, February). *Toward a new understanding of non-academic student support: Four mechanisms encouraging positive student outcomes in the community college* (Working Paper No. 28). New York, NY: Community College Research Center, Teachers College, Columbia University.

Lee, J. B. (2010). Student outcomes by state. *Data Notes: Keeping Informed About Achieving the Dream Data, 5*(6), 1–4.

Lotkowski, V. A., Robbins, S. B., & Noeth, R. J. (2004). *The role of academic and non-academic factors in improving college retention*. ACT Policy Report. Iowa City, IA: American College Testing ACT.

Marti, C. N. (2008). Dimensions of student engagement in American community colleges: Using the community college student report in research and practice. *Community College Journal of Research and Practice, 33*(1), 1–24.

Miller, J. W., Janz, J. C., & Chen, C. (2007). The retention impact of a first-year seminar on students with varying pre-college academic performance. *Journal of the First Year Experience & Students in Transition, 19*(1), 47–62.

Morest, V. S., & Jenkins, D. (2007, April). *Institutional research and the culture of evidence at community colleges* (Report No. 1 in the Achieving the Dream *Culture of Evidence Series*). New York, NY: Community College Research Center, Teachers College, Columbia University.

Padgett, R. D., Salisbury, M. H., An, B. P., & Pascarella, E. T. (2010). Required, practical, or unnecessary? An examination and demonstration of propensity score matching using longitudinal secondary data. In T. A. Seifert (Ed.), *New Directions for Institutional Research—Assessment Supplement: S2. Longitudinal assessment for institutional improvement* (pp. 29–42). San Francisco, CA: Jossey-Bass.

Pascarella, E. T., & Terenzini, P. T. (2005). *How college affects students: A third decade of research*. San Francisco, CA: Jossey-Bass.

Porter, S. R., & Swing, R. L. (2006). Understanding how first-year seminars affect persistence. *Research in Higher Education, 47*(1), 89–109.

Prentice, M., & Robinson, G. (2010). *Improving student learning outcomes with service learning*. Washington, DC: American Association of Community Colleges. Retrieved from http://www.aacc.nche.edu/Resources/aaccprograms/horizons/Documents/slorb_jan2010.pdf

Price, E. (2010). *Early alert at Sinclair Community College*. Retrieved from http://ccctitle3.files.wordpress.com/2009/05/earlyalertnacada.ppt

Reason, R. D., Cox, B. E., McIntosh, K., & Terenzini, P. T. (2010, May). *Deep learning as an individual, conditional, and contextual influence on first-year student outcomes*. Paper presented at the Annual Forum of the Association for Institutional Research, Chicago, IL.

Scrivener, S., Bloom, D., LeBlanc, A., Paxson, C., Rouse, C. E., & Sommo, C. (2008). *A good start: Two-year effects of a freshmen learning community program at Kingsborough Community College*. New York, NY: MDRC.

Scrivener, S., & Coghlan, E. (2011). *Opening doors to student success: A synthesis of findings from an evaluation at six community colleges*. New York, NY: MDRC.

Scrivener, S., Sommo, C., & Collado, H. (2009). *Getting back on track: effects of a community college program for probationary students*. New York, NY: MDRC.

South Texas College. (2006, Fall). *A comparative analysis of the STC case management advising program for first time in college students, 1*(2). Retrieved from http://ras.southtexascollege.edu/files/Research-Brief-Beacon-Case-Management-Impact-Study-revised-10082010.pdf

Stupka, E. (1993). *An evaluation of the short term and long term impact a student success course has on academic performance and persistence* (Research Report). Retrieved from http://www.eric.ed.gov/ERICWebPortal/contentdelivery/servlet/ERICServlet?accno=ED364300

Tobolowsky, B. F. (2008). *2006 National Survey of First-Year Seminars: Continuing innovations in the collegiate curriculum*. The First-Year Experience Monograph Series No. 51. Columbia: National Resource Center for The First-Year Experience and Students in Transition, University of South Carolina.

Tobolowsky, B. F., Cox, B. E., & Wagner, M. T. (2005). *Exploring the evidence: Reporting research on first-year seminars* (Vol. III). The First-Year Experience, Monograph Series No. 42. Columbia: The University of South Carolina.

University 101. (2010). *History of the first university seminar & the University 101 program*. University of South Carolina. Retrieved from http://www.sc.edu/univ101/aboutus/history.html

Upcraft, M. L., Gardner, J. N., Barefoot, B. O., & Associates. (2005). *Challenging and supporting the first-year student: A handbook for improving the first year of college*. San Francisco, CA: Jossey-Bass.

Wahlstrom, C. M. (1993). Genesee Community College. In B. O. Barefoot (Ed.), *Exploring the evidence: Reporting outcomes of freshman seminars* (pp. 15–16). Columbia:

National Resource Center for The Freshman Year Experience, University of South Carolina.

Weiss, M. J., Visher, M. G., & Wathington, H. (2010). *Learning communities for students in developmental reading: An impact study at Hillsborough Community College.* New York, NY: MDRC.

Zeidenberg, M., Jenkins, D., & Calcagno, J. C. (2007, June). *Do student success courses actually help community college students succeed?* (Issue Brief No. 36). New York, NY: Community College Research Center, Teachers College, Columbia University.

TRUDY BERS *was formerly the executive director of Institutional Research, Curriculum and Planning at Oakton Community College in Des Plaines, Illinois. She is now president of The Bers Group.*

DONNA YOUNGER *was formerly the dean of Academic Services at Oakton Community College in Des Plaines, Illinois. She is now the principal partner at Younger Directions.*

NEW DIRECTIONS FOR INSTITUTIONAL RESEARCH • DOI: 10.1002/ir

INDEX

AAC&U. *See* Association of American Colleges and Universities (AAC&U)

AACC. *See* American Association of Community Colleges (AACC)

Academic Challenge megascale: leadership effects on 43, 45; outcomes, significant differences of, for White and African-American students, 46–50; overview, 37–40; psychological well-being, effects on, 43, 45; questions comprising, 42

Achieving the Dream (AtD), 78, 85–86

Alexander, J. S., 9, 53, 58, 66–67

Alfonso, M., 77, 82

Allen, W. R., 38

American Association of Community Colleges (AACC), 85, 90

An, B. P., 88

Association of American Colleges and Universities (AAC&U), 9

Astin, A. W., 14, 21, 40, 55

Astin, H. S., 40

AtD. *See* Achieving the Dream (AtD)

Augustana College (IL), 21

Babbie, E., 56

Bailey, T. R., 77, 82

Banta, T. W., 14–16

Barefoot, B. O., 7, 11–12, 15–16, 53, 66–67, 78, 83–84

Barlow, E., 62

Barron's, 26

Bauer, K. W., 23–24

Baxter Magolda, M. B., 10, 38

Bean, J. P., 55

Bennett, J. S., 23–24

Berry, T. R., 54

Bers, T., 2, 77, 93

Black, K. E., 14–16

Blaich, C. F., 37, 48

Blimling, G. S., 37

Bloom, D., 82

Boudreau, C., 54

Brame, R., 43

Bringle, R. G., 20

Briscoe, K., 49

Brock, T., 88

Bruhn, J. W., 54

Cabrera, A. F., 57

Cabrera, N. L., 24, 31

Calcagno, J. C., 81

Carini, R. M., 31

CCRC. *See* Community College Research Center (CCRC)

CCSSE. *See* Community College Survey of Student Engagement (CCSSE)

Center for Postsecondary Research, 9

Center for Vocational Reflection (Augustana College), 21

Chappell, C., 83

Chen, C., 81

Chickering, A. W., 37, 48

Cho, S. W., 81

Christie, N. G., 63

CIRP. *See* Cooperative Institutional Research Program (CIRP)

CIRP Constructs, 57

Clayton-Pedersen, A. R., 38

Clemson University, 24

Clery, S., 90

Coghlan, E., 79, 84

Collado, H., 84

College Student Experiences Questionnaire, 37

Community College Leadership Program, 9

Community College Research Center (CCRC), 81

Community College Survey of Student Engagement (CCSSE), 9, 85, 90

Cooperative Institutional Research Program (CIRP), 11, 13, 55, 57

Couper, M. P., 44

Course content, discussed with students outside of class, 60–65; first-year seminars, effect of, 62, 64–65; gender, effect of, 61–62; housing, effect of, 62–64

Cox, B. E., 81, 83

Crisp, G., 62
Crissman Ishler, J. L., 6
Cruce, T. M., 37, 48
Cutright, M., 11–12

DeAngelo, L., 2, 53, 57, 62, 63, 66
DeAntoni, T., 23–24
DEEP. *See* Documenting Effective Educational Practice (DEEP) project
Deep learning, 25; approaches to, 34
Dey, E. L., 56
Dinham, S. M., 63
Diverse Experiences megascale, 40
Documenting Effective Educational Practice (DEEP) project, 9, 83
Doetkott, C. D., 54

Eagan, M. K., 24, 31
EBI. *See* Educational Benchmarking Inc. (EBI)
Education gains, 35
Educational Benchmarking Inc. (EBI), 9
El-Khawas, E., 12
Ewell, P. T., 6
Eyler, J., 21

Farnsworth, N., 21
First-year assessment: conceptual considerations for, 5–17; direct and indirect measures of, 14–16; locally developed instruments for, 11–13; mixed methods for, 8–11; national surveys for, 11–13; objectives of, 6–8; outcomes of, 6–8; overview, 5–6; qualitative method for, 8–11; quantitative method for, 8–11
First-year college experiences, retention and: background on, 54–55; course content, discussed with students outside of class, 63–71; faculty interactions, 65; financial concerns, 65; first-year curriculum, 58; first-year seminar participation, 54–55; logistic model, predicting intent to persist, 59–60, 73–75; overview, 53–54; variables, description of, 70–72
First-year experience (FYE) programs at community colleges, 77–91: academic advising, 84; challenges of conducting research on, 89–90; characteristics of, 78–79; collaboration in, 89; core com-
ponents of, 79–85; data or information presentation, 89; early alert systems, 83–84; first-year seminars, 80–81; four-year colleges, comparison to, 80; identification of data, 87–88; integrating research and program delivery, strategies for, 86–89; learning communities, 81–82; national initiatives on, 85–86; orientation, 82–83; outcome data of, 88; overview, 77; part-time enrollment in, 90; program objectives, 87; research on, 78–79; services, identification of, 88; student attributes, 87; student engagement, 84–85; Student Life Skills course, 81; transient student populations in, 90
First-Year Initiative (FYI) survey, 9
First-year seminars: course content, discussed with students outside of class, 63–71; FYE programs and, 80–81; participation in, 54–55
Fleming, J., 14
Foundations of Excellence®, 78, 85–86
Fowler, F. J., Jr., 44
Franke, R., 62, 63, 66
Frederick Community College, 83
Freed, J. E., 6
Freshman Survey, 9

Gabelnick, F., 22
Gallini, S. M., 21
Gamson, Z. F., 37, 48
Garcia, N., 14
Gardner, J. N., 9, 11–12, 53, 58, 66–67
Giles, D., 28
Gilmartin, S. K., 55, 57
Gonyea, R. M., 2, 14–15, 19, 26, 35
Good Teaching megascale: leadership effects on, 43–44; outcomes, significant differences of, for White and African-American students, 45–46, 48–50; overview, 37–40; psychological well-being, effects on, 43–44; questions comprising, 41
Goodman, K. M., 2, 10, 37–38, 48, 51
Gregerman, S. R., 24
Groves, R. M., 44

Hagedorn, L. S., 57
Haladyna, T. M., 14
Handel, D. D., 55

Hansen, M. J., 53
Hatcher, J. A., 20
Healy, M., 23–24
HERI. *See* Higher Education Research Institute (HERI)
Herzog, S., 57, 65
High-impact practices, 19–35; deep approaches to learning, 25, 34; first-year experience, satisfaction with, 26, 35; institutional characteristics, 28; learning communities in, 21–23; living-learning programs, 22; measures, 25–26; outcomes of, 28–31; overview, 19–20; participation in, 26–29; self-reported gains, 25–26, 35; service learning, 20–21; student characteristics, 26–28; undergraduate research, 23–24
Higher Education Research Institute (HERI), 55–56, 78
Higher order learning, 25, 34
Hillsborough Community College, 82
Hobsons, T., 83
Hosmer, D. W., 57
Huba, M. E., 6
Hunt, P., 54
Hunter, A.-B., 23–24
Hunter, M. S., 64
Hurtado, S., 24, 31, 38, 53, 62, 63, 66

Ikeda, E. K., 21, 55
Illinois Campus Compact, 21
Indiana University Purdue University-Indianapolis (IUPUI), 22–23
Integrated Postsecondary Education Data System (IPEDS), 56
Integrative learning, 25, 34
IPEDS. *See* Integrated Postsecondary Education Data System (IPEDS)
IUPUI. *See* Indiana University Purdue University-Indianapolis (IUPUI)

Janz, J. C., 81
Jenkins, A., 23–24
Jenkins, D., 81, 86
Jones, E. A., 14–16
Jonides, J., 24

Kanoy, K. W., 54
Kardash, C. M., 23–24
Karp, M. M., 79, 81
Keup, J. R., 2, 5, 7, 10, 13, 15–16, 18

Keyes, C., 41
Kilgo, C. A., 2, 5, 18
King, P. M., 10, 21, 38
Kingsborough Community College, 82
Kinkead, J., 23
Kinzie, J., 9, 37, 48
Koch, A. K., 7, 15–16
Krishnan, T., 56
Kromrey, J., 54
Kuh, G. D., 9, 19–20, 25, 31, 37, 48, 53, 55
Kurotsuchi Inkelas, K., 22

Laufgraben, J. L., 22
Laursen, S., 23–24
Leadership outcomes: academic challenge on, effects of, 45, 47; for White and African-American students, 43–48; good teaching on, effects of, 44, 46
Learning: deep, 25, 34; higher order, 25, 34; integrative, 25, 34; reflective, 25, 34; service, 20–21, 27, 29; surface, 25
Learning communities, 21–23; FYE programs and, 81–82; participation in, 27, 29
LeBlanc, A., 82
Lee, J. B., 90
Lemeshow, S., 57
Lepkowski, J. M., 44
Lerner, J. S., 24
Leskes, A., 7
Lin, C. H., 53
Lin, M. H., 24, 31
Linder, C. W., 64
Lopatto, D., 23
Lopez, M., 24, 31
Lotkowski, V. A., 83
Love G. A., 22

Mabrouk, P. A., 23
MacGregor, J., 22
Maki, P., 6, 14
Marti, C. N., 85
Marton, F., 25
Matthews, R. S., 22
Mayhew, M. J., 21, 49
Mazerolle, P., 43
McIntosh, K., 83
McLachlan, G. J., 56
Merriam, S. B., 8

Milem, J. F., 38
Miller, A., 26
Miller, J. W., 81
Miller, R., 7
Moely, B. E., 21
Morest, V. S., 86
Morris, L. V., 11–12

Nagda, B. A., 24
National Center for Postsecondary Research's Learning Communities Demonstration, 82
National Conferences on Undergraduate Research, 23
National Resource Center for The First-Year Experience and Students in Transition, 7, 13, 78
National Survey of Efforts to Improve Undergraduate Student Success and Retention, 15
National Survey of First-Year Seminars (2009), 7–8, 10
National Survey of Student Engagement (NSSE), 9, 19–20, 37; learning communities, data for, 22–23; service learning, data for, 21; undergraduate research, data for, 24
Nelson Laird, T. F., 25
Nigro, G., 21
Noeth, R. J., 83
Nora, A., 57, 62
NSSE. See National Survey of Student Engagement (NSSE)

Padgett, R. D., 2, 3, 7, 10, 13, 15–16, 88
Palomba, C. A., 14, 16
Park, J., 24, 31
Pascarella, E. T., 14–15, 37, 48–49, 53–54, 57, 58, 81, 88
Paternoster, R., 43
Paxson, C., 82
Personal gains, 35
Peters, K., 23
Peterson, T., 57
Pike, G. R., 53–54
Piquero, A., 43
Porter, S. R., 58, 64, 81
Positive Peer Interactions megascale, 39–40
Practical gains, 35
Prentice, M., 85

Price, E., 83
Profiles of American Colleges, 26
Pryor, J., 57, 62, 63, 66
Psychological well-being outcomes: academic challenge on, effects of, 45, 47; for White and African-American students, 43–48; good teaching on, effects of, 44, 46

Reason, R. D., 83
Reflective learning, 25, 34
Research with faculty, 24, 27, 28; participation in, 27, 29
Rhodes, T. L., 7, 9
Robbins, S. B., 83
Robinson, G., 85
Rocconi, L. M., 53
Rouse, C. E., 82
Ryff, C., 41, 43

Salisbury, M. H., 88
Säljö, R., 25
Sax, L. J., 55, 57
Scales of Psychological Well-being (SPWB), 41–43
Schnell, C. A., 54
Schroeder, C. C., 11–12, 54
Schuh, J. H., 5, 9, 12, 37, 48
Schwarts, S. W., 11–12
Schwartz, M. J., 25
Scrivener, S., 79, 82, 84
Seifert, T. A., 10, 38
Self-reported gains, 25–26, 35
SENSE. See Survey of Entering Student Engagement (SENSE)
Service learning, 20–21; benefits of, 55; participation in, 27, 29
Seymour, E., 23–24
Sharkness, J., 57
Shmotkin, D., 41
Shoup, R., 25
Siegel, M. J., 5
Simpson, E. L., 8
Sinclair Community College, 83
Singer, E., 44
SLS. See Student Life Skills (SLS)
Smith, B. L., 22
Social gains, 35
Socially Responsible Leadership Scale (SRLS), 40
Sommo, C., 82, 84

SPWB. *See* Scales of Psychological Well-being (SPWB)
SRLS. *See* Socially Responsible Leadership Scale (SRLS)
Stage, F. K., 43, 49
Strumph, G., 54
Student Life Skills (SLS), 81
Student satisfaction, 35; with first-year experience, 26
Stupka, E., 81
Surface learning, 25
Survey of Entering Student Engagement (SENSE), 85–86
Swing, R. L., 1, 5–6, 11–12, 58, 64, 81

Terenzini, P. T., 53–54, 58, 83, 85
Tinto, V., 53–54
Tobolowsky, B. F., 80–81
Tokuno, K., 22
Tourangeau, R., 44
Tran, S., 62, 63, 66
Tukibayeva, M., 2, 19, 35
Tyree, T., 40

Upcraft, M. L., 5–6, 11–12, 53, 66–67, 78, 83–84

Valid Assessment of Learning in Undergraduate Education (VALUE), 9

VALUE. *See* Valid Assessment of Learning in Undergraduate Education (VALUE)
Visher, M. G., 82
Vogelgesang, L. J., 21, 55
Von Hippel, W., 24

Wabash National Study of Liberal Arts Education, 2, 9, 37–40, 49
Wagner, M. T., 81
Wahlstrom, C. M., 81
Wathington, H., 82
Weiss, M. J., 82
Whitt, E. J., 9, 37, 48
Wolfe, J., 63
Wolniak, G. C., 37, 48

Yee, J. A., 21, 55
YFCY survey. *See* Your First College Year (YFCY) survey
Younger, D., 2, 77, 93
Your First College Year (YFCY) survey, 9, 55–56

Zeidenberg, M., 81
Zeller, W. J., 63
Zhao, C.-M., 31
Zlotkowski, E., 20–21